# BEETHOVEN

*The 35 Piano Sonatas*, Volume 2
*Die 35 Klaviersonaten*, Band 2

# BEETHOVEN

## *The 35 Piano Sonatas*

### *Die 35 Klaviersonaten*

Volume/Band 2

---

Edited by/Herausgegeben von
BARRY COOPER

Fingering by/Fingersatz von
DAVID WARD

The Associated Board of the Royal Schools of Music

First published in 2007 by
The Associated Board of the Royal Schools of Music (Publishing) Limited
24 Portland Place, London W1B 1LU, United Kingdom

© 2007 by The Associated Board of the Royal Schools of Music
A CIP catalogue for this book is available from The British Library.
Printed in England by Caligraving Ltd, Thetford, Norfolk.
Reprinted in 2008.

Music setting/Notensatz: Andrew Jones
Text setting/Textsatz: Hope Services (Abingdon) Ltd, England
German translation/Deutsche Übersetzung: Albrecht Dümling

Cover by Vermillion Design, incorporating Beethoven's signature from a letter to
Franz Brentano, 12 November 1821 (Beethoven-Haus, Bonn).
Umschlag von Vermillion Design, unter Verwendung von Beethovens Unterschrift aus
einem Brief an Franz Brentano vom 12. November 1821 (Beethoven-Haus, Bonn).

# CONTENTS / INHALT

## Volume / Band 1

---

# Volume/Band 2

---

Op. 22, B flat major/B-Dur

Op. 26, A flat major/As-Dur

Op. 27 No. 1 (*quasi una fantasia*), E flat major/Es-Dur

Op. 27 No. 2 (*quasi una fantasia*, 'Moonlight'/'Mondschein'),
C sharp minor/cis-Moll

Op. 28 ('Pastorale'), D major/D-Dur

Op. 31 No. 1, G major/G-Dur

Op. 31 No. 2, D minor/d-Moll

Op. 31 No. 3, E flat major/Es-Dur

(Op. 49: Volume/Band 1)

Op. 53 ('Waldstein'), C major/C-Dur

Op. 54, F major/F-Dur

# Volume/Band 3

---

Op. 57 ('Appassionata'), F minor/f-Moll

Op. 78, F sharp major/Fis-Dur

Op. 79, G major/G-Dur

Op. 81a (*Das Lebewohl*, 'Les adieux'), E flat major/Es-Dur

Op. 90, E minor/e-Moll

Op. 101, A major/A-Dur

Op. 106 ('Hammerklavier'), B flat major/B-Dur

Op. 109, E major/E-Dur

Op. 110, A flat major/As-Dur

Op. 111, C minor/c-Moll

A miniature portrait of Beethoven, painted by Christian Horneman (1765–1844) in 1802 (not 1803 as often stated: see Brandenburg ed., *Briefwechsel*, No. 197, note 2). It is considered the best likeness of Beethoven from before 1812. In 1804 Beethoven sent the painting to his friend Stephan von Breuning as a gesture of reconciliation after a quarrel, and it remained with the Breuning family for many years.
(Beethoven-Haus, Bonn)

Ein Miniatur-Porträt Beethovens, gemalt von Christian Horneman (1765–1844) im Jahre 1802 (nicht 1803, wie oft angegeben: s. Brandenburg Hg., *Briefwechsel*, Nr. 197, Anm. 2). Es gilt als die ähnlichste Darstellung Beethovens vor 1812. Im Jahr 1804 schickte Beethoven das Gemälde seinem Freund Stephan von Breuning als Geste der Versöhnung nach einem Streit und es blieb für viele Jahre im Besitz der Breuning-Familie.
(Beethoven-Haus, Bonn)

# INTRODUCTION

## EDITORIAL PRINCIPLES AND SOURCES

Beethoven published 35 piano sonatas in the course of his life. They span almost the whole of his career, from three issued in 1783 at the age of 12 to the magnificent C minor sonata Op.111 of 1822. They have remained unequalled to this day, and form a cornerstone of the pianist's repertory. Numerous editions of them have been published, but in most of the older ones little attempt was made to transmit Beethoven's intentions exactly, and the editors often adapted the printed text to suit the tastes and performing styles of their own age (though the notes themselves were rarely altered). Today, however, it is widely believed that Beethoven's piano sonatas (like other music of past centuries) are best performed as the composer intended at the time, as far as this is knowable, rather than in some distorted form that incorporates later performing styles. One reason is that to do otherwise is to perform something other than a 'sonata by Beethoven': it would be a sonata by Beethoven as revised by someone else, be they editor, arranger or performer. Even slight deviations that are known to be contrary to what was intended are no different in principle, but only in degree, from the most far-fetched of arrangements. Although such arrangements may have considerable merit, they can no longer be described as sonatas by Beethoven – the purity of the composition has become contaminated. Moreover, it is extremely unlikely that any such revisions would be improvements on Beethoven's ideas; the result would almost certainly be not just different but inferior.

This is not to say that there is only one correct manner of performance for each sonata, for the music admits many interpretations, and it is essential that pianists impart something of their own feelings and personalities in their performances. Nor did Beethoven's view of what might constitute an ideal performance necessarily remain the same throughout his life. However, it is important not to introduce any performance features that are known to contravene directly his intentions and expectations, even though these intentions admit a certain flexibility of approach.

The present edition uses these principles as its starting point. It aims firstly to present the musical text precisely as Beethoven intended it (as far as this is possible), through a detailed reassessment of all the relevant sources, and secondly to give sufficient explanation of the meaning of his notation; for, contrary to popular belief, notation has evolved considerably since 1800, and certain unwritten assumptions of the period have to be spelt out today. All 35 sonatas are included (most other editions unjustifiably omit the first three), and they are presented in chronological order of composition, so that the development of Beethoven's style can be more easily seen. (There are two slight exceptions: Op. 49 Nos. 1 and 2 are presented together in numerical order before Op. 7, although No. 1 was apparently composed after No. 2 and probably also after Op. 7; and Op. 78 appears before Op. 79 although it was probably composed immediately after it.)

When using a modern edition of music written many years ago, pianists need to be aware of the history behind the notes they see. With Beethoven's sonatas, the notes that originated in his mind were often tried out on the piano in various forms before being written down at all. He also made numerous rough drafts in the form of sketches, before a final score – the **autograph** – was written out. Details in this were then amended in various ways. Next a professional copyist usually made a **fair copy**, which was checked and annotated by Beethoven, perhaps with a few further revisions. The copy (or the autograph itself) was then sent to the printers, who engraved a set of plates and printed a proof copy. This was generally sent to Beethoven for checking, before a run of, say, 100 corrected copies was printed – the first **impression**. If further errors were noticed, additional corrections might be made before a second and perhaps third impression were run off. It follows, therefore, that none of these sources is likely to contain a definitive version. The autograph might contain notational errors – for example, Beethoven occasionally forgot to insert a vital accidental – and it would not include any last-minute revisions inserted into the copyist's score. But this score, while including these and perhaps the accidentals previously missing, might also contain copying errors overlooked by Beethoven. So, too, might the printed edition, particularly if Beethoven had not been given the chance to check it. Thus claims by some modern editions that they are 'Urtext' (literally, 'original text') are misleading, since there probably never was an original text entirely free from errors.

In certain sonatas the problems are compounded by a later edition, engraved and issued independently with Beethoven's co-operation by a different publisher, and containing slightly different readings in places. Furthermore, in most of the sonatas at least one source – autograph score or copyist's fair copy – is now lost; indeed all that remains for many sonatas, especially the early ones, is the original edition, which may contain significant errors. The concept of an 'original edition', too, is fraught with problems that are not always recognized by modern editors. Several copies or **exemplars** may survive from the first impression, but several more, seemingly identical to them at first sight, may come from a slightly modified later impression. Others may come from a later **issue**, where the same set of plates has been used by a different publisher; only if a fresh set of plates is used, by either the same or more often a different publisher, can one refer to it as a later **edition**.

Most of these other early editions, of which there are many, were simply copied from existing ones. They invariably introduce fresh errors, while any corrections they include are likely to be of obvious errors. It can normally be assumed that the publishers had no direct contact with Beethoven about their publication, and so these variant readings have no authority. Consequently, all such editions have been disregarded for present purposes unless there is clear evidence that Beethoven had some direct connection with them. For editions where he was involved, however, a modern editor should ideally consult every known exemplar, in case it shows a significant and authentic variant. This has not been feasible for the present edition, and it would scarcely have affected the final text anyway; but at least two exemplars have normally been scrutinized – the one reproduced in Brian Jeffery's facsimile edition (see References below) and at least one more – rather than just a single specimen. (Jeffery's facsimiles, incidentally, were somewhat cleaned up during reproduction, with random spots removed. Unfortunately a few staccato marks etc. also disappeared during this process, creating occasional minor deviations from the original edition.)

Where Beethoven made intentional changes at a very late stage, it is normally the latest version – the *Fassung letzter Hand* as it is known in German – that is regarded as the official one. Sometimes, however, it is unclear whether last-minute changes are the result of oversight or deliberate attempts at improvement. Any modern edition, therefore, is bound to include small amounts of editorial guesswork in such places. The present edition gives the readings that are believed to represent his final intentions (as far as these can be established), while indicating in the Commentary those places where there is room for substantial doubt. To give full reasons for each editorial choice would be impracticable, but each decision is the result of careful consideration of both stylistic and textual factors, and attempts to reflect the balance of probabilities. It must be stressed that where such uncertainty exists it nearly always concerns minor details such as the length or presence of slurs and crescendo marks; only occasionally are the actual notes in doubt.

## Performance Practice

Obtaining an accurate musical text through careful study of the sources is an essential first step towards performing a Beethoven sonata, but even if every notational detail is correctly reproduced on the piano a satisfactory performance is not guaranteed. In his day there were also many unwritten conventions that were expected to be observed in any performance. Some of these are still familiar today while others have to be relearned. The latter type have been the subject of much research in recent years, and literature on the subject has become quite extensive. Particularly noteworthy are books by William S. Newman and Sandra P. Rosenblum (see References below), to which the reader is referred for more details on the matters discussed here. Some performance questions, however, are still matters of dispute, and will perhaps never result in clear-cut answers. In the present edition each sonata is provided with detailed editorial notes offering informed guidance about many of the more problematical passages, where either the text or its interpretation is in some way ambiguous. This guidance will inevitably include a subjective element, however, and performers are entitled to reject the editor's opinions if they have sufficient reason.

### Instruments

When Beethoven published his earliest piano sonatas in the 1780s and 90s, the instruments for which he wrote were very different from the modern piano – so different, in fact, that they are sometimes referred to nowadays as fortepianos to distinguish them. They had a quieter tone and lighter touch, sounds died away much quicker, the sustaining pedal (where present) created less resonance, there was more contrast between registers, and the compass was a mere five octaves (*FF* to $f^3$). It is not actually essential to use a fortepiano in order to play the early sonatas effectively. For a start, there was a great variety of sound between different pianos, yet Beethoven did not reject any type as positively unsuitable for his music (nor did he find any that were wholly satisfactory). Nevertheless, pianists should try to become familiar with the sonority of early pianos, through recordings or, better still, first-hand acquaintance. Such instruments, which possess many beautiful and distinctive qualities that later manufacturers tended to smooth out, provide great insights into the kind of sound world that Beethoven envisaged for his sonatas. These sonorities can then to some extent be reproduced on a modern instrument.

During Beethoven's lifetime manufacturers were constantly experimenting with ways of making their instruments bigger and louder. By the 1820s the compass of many was six and a half octaves, and modifications such as thicker strings, stronger frames and larger hammers made them sound much more like instruments of today; but they still show significant differences in tone and touch from any modern grand or upright. The pitch of instruments tended to be slightly lower than today. It was not absolutely fixed, however, and the difference was generally less than a semitone, so that modern concert pitch ($a^1$ = 440) is perfectly acceptable. Equal temperament was not invariable, but something close to it was normal, enabling rapid enharmonic modulation to remote keys, while any inequalities tended to enhance the individuality of each key.

### Pedalling

Beethoven rarely marks any pedalling, and there is none at all in the early sonatas. His pupil Carl Czerny, however, tells us that Beethoven used the pedals far more than is indicated (Czerny 1970, p.16). Thus modern performers should not feel inhibited about using the sustaining pedal where there is no marking, especially in the later sonatas (use of the pedal probably increased considerably during the course of Beethoven's lifetime, and its sustaining effect tended to become more pronounced). On the other hand, the temptation to use it too extensively, so that the music becomes swathed in a wash of almost continual background sonority, should be resisted. It is in fact possible to give a convincing performance of the early sonatas (at least up to Opus 10 inclusive) without any pedal at all, and it is instructive to experiment with this, since the player is forced to think more deeply about matters of phrasing, articulation and fingering. Where Beethoven did indicate pedalling, whether with the sustaining pedal or the soft pedal, it was sometimes to create an unusual effect. These effects are discussed in detail in the commentaries on the relevant sonatas.

### Tempo and the Metronome

Before the invention of the metronome it was impossible for a composer to indicate a tempo reliably. Clues could be given through terms such as *allegro* and *andante*, and also through the choice of the time signature **C** or **₵** (the latter implying a faster tempo), but much had to be left to chance, as Beethoven himself lamented in a letter of 1812. Shortly after this, however, the metronome was invented, and he was the first major composer to use it. He gave metronome marks for only one of his sonatas – the 'Hammerklavier', Op. 106 – and these are rather fast (Donald Tovey describes that for the first movement as 'impossible'). Many of his metronome marks for his quartets and symphonies, however, also seem on the fast side, and although a few are plainly erroneous, others seem fast mainly because speeds in music in general tended to slow down during the decades after his death, so that people became accustomed to hearing much of his music at a slightly slower pace than he intended, in both quick and slow movements.

In the absence of Beethoven's own metronome marks, the nearest we can come to his intentions is to follow the advice of his pupil Czerny, who studied many of the sonatas with Beethoven himself and later wrote down recommended speeds on the basis of what he could remember. Some of these may also seem rather fast, thus implicitly confirming that Beethoven's figures were not the result of error. (It is interesting to note that, concerning the first movement of the 'Hammerklavier', Czerny does not regard Beethoven's tempo as impossible but merely the cause of 'difficulty' and the need for 'attentive practice'! See Czerny 1970, p. 64/54.) Czerny's metronome marks are reproduced here in the commentaries, but in many movements he gave more than one figure on different occasions (Rosenblum 1988, pp. 329–30, 355–61), in which case both his fastest and slowest speeds are given here (unless otherwise indicated). It is important to remember that these are only rough guides, and can be adjusted to allow for such factors as the surrounding acoustics, the quality of the instrument and the ability of the player. Moreover, metronome marks were not intended to be followed rigidly throughout a movement – they are just an indication of an initial speed. There is abundant evidence from Czerny and others that, although Beethoven expected pianists to play in essentially strict time, some flexibility is admissible, and there are many contexts in which the music can be temporarily slowed down or (less often) speeded up. Passages where Czerny recommends a ritardando include those just before the return of the main theme, before a pause, before a new tempo, and at gentle cadences (see Barth 1992, especially pp. 74–7, 85–6). Tempo flexibility or 'rubato' can be applied to whole phrases or sections, note groups, or just individual notes or chords. It should, of course, always be used to heighten the expression, and not just as arbitrary variation of tempo. The same applies to other unwritten devices that seem to have been common in Beethoven's day, including playing the r.h. slightly after the l.h. in cantabile melodies, and adding arpeggiation on slow chords.

## Dynamics

Since Beethoven's pianos were considerably quieter than modern ones, there was less scope for tone gradation, and fewer dynamic levels were recognized. The sonatas use only four basic ones – **pp**, **p**, **f** and **ff** – plus various combinations such as **sf**, **fp** and *cresc.*; thus the difference between **p** and **f** is less than would be the case in later music where **mp** and **mf** are widely used. The sign **f** occasionally appears as a slightly less emphatic alternative to **sf**, but this usage is generally clear from the context. The first sonata to use **ppp** is Op. 7, but this sign remains very rare, while **mf** (see Op. 101) and **mp** (see Op. 111, where it is written in full as 'mezzo piano') are even rarer. The term *mezza voce* also appears occasionally and may be roughly synonymous with **mp** or **p**. The sign **sfp** indicates an accent followed by an immediate **p**; but where the context is already soft, the accent itself should probably be less than a full **sf**. Another sign used is *rinforzando* or *rinf.*, meaning 'reinforcing' or 'strengthening'. Although theorists were not in complete agreement about its use, Beethoven seems to have intended it as a milder form of **sf**, usually applied to a single note or chord but occasionally to more. Crescendo and diminuendo are sometimes notated as hairpins. The diminuendo hairpin often follows **sf** or other loud dynamic mark. Where it appears on its own, however, whether on one note or extending to more than one, it seems to denote an accent (less strong than **sf**, since it can be used along with this) plus diminuendo to the previous dynamic level.

## Slurs and articulation

When approaching the problem of Beethoven's slurs, one must remember that in the 18th century the normal touch was a detached one. For instance Daniel Gottlob Türk, writing in 1789, stated: 'With the notes that are to be played in the usual manner, i.e. neither staccato nor slurred, the finger is lifted from the keyboard a little earlier than the duration of the note demands' (*Klavierschule*, p. 356, cited from Barth 1992, p. 42, translation altered). By varying the moment at which the finger is lifted, from a near staccato to almost complete legato, great subtlety of articulation and expression could be achieved. If the composer wanted a note to be joined to the next by a full legato, he used a short slur to indicate this; if he wanted a whole passage played legato, he used a long slur, which is nowadays often wrongly referred to as a 'phrase mark' – an anachronistic concept. Beethoven used these long legato marks far more than his predecessors, but there are places where there is no articulation mark. Here a detached touch, of the type described by Türk, should be used unless there is good reason to do otherwise (for example, if a similar passage immediately before was slurred). This rule does not necessarily apply to Beethoven's last works, by which time legato touch was becoming increasingly the norm.

Türk also mentions that the first note under a slur should be 'very gently (almost imperceptibly) accented' (Barth 1992, p. 111). This advice applies particularly to short slurs over two or three notes, but should also be borne in mind for longer ones, where it is also often appropriate. As for the last note under a slur, there is some uncertainty about how often this may be joined to the next note. The situation is not much clarified by Beethoven's remark to Karl Holz in August 1825: 'It is not all the same whether it is like this ♫ or like this ♫ ' (Brandenburg ed., 1996–8, No. 2032). Beethoven is here referring to string music, where the difference between the two cases is quite clear since it affects the bowing. In piano music the difference is much less conspicuous, but it should still be observed. This becomes evident through a comparison of excerpts from two of his sonatas:

Op. 14 No. 2.III

Op. 49 No. 2.II

In the first case each three-note group is a single gesture, to be played legato and tailing off on the third note. In the second case, however, the staccato notes should probably be slightly more emphasized than in the first example; they should also be very slightly detached from the previous note, if the speed of the piece and the action of the piano permit.

With short slurs, covering only two, three or occasionally four notes, the last note in the group should be shortened. Thus in the following example, the second note of each pair should be somewhat staccato, whether or not it is followed by a repeated note. It might also be played very slightly early:

Op. 31 No. 2.I

With longer slurs, however, the last note does not need to be detached from what follows. It was normally inconvenient to draw very long slurs since they would either lose their shape or interfere with the stave above or below, and so they were customarily broken up into shorter ones. As Czerny remarked, 'When smaller slurs appear separately over two or three notes, the second or third note will be somewhat clipped [*abgestossen*]…But when slurs appear over more notes, though separated, they should be regarded as if it were only one, and no break should be evident' (cited from Barth 1992, pp. 104–5, translation altered). Thus two or more adjacent slurs of more than two or three notes each should be played the same as one continuous slur, if Czerny's advice is to be trusted (though it was written many years after Beethoven's early sonatas). In this case, several inconsistencies of slurring between exposition and recapitulation become mere notational variants. The present edition, however, retains the original slurs to show the kinds of inconsistencies that result, and to enable pianists to decide whether particular breaks in slurs are of significance for the performer. It also preserves any irregular beaming of quavers and semiquavers in the original, since this may provide subtle hints about how Beethoven perceived certain groups of notes.

## Staccato

The main problem with Beethoven's staccatos derives from his use of both dots and dashes. In his letter of 1825 cited above he instructed his copyist, 'Where · · is above the note ı ı must

not be put instead and vice versa.' His scores are not always clear, however. He normally used vertical dashes, but these can be so short as to resemble dots, creating apparent inconsistencies between parallel passages. Some modern authorities therefore claim that all his staccato marks are intended to be dashes except those under slurs, where he seems always to have preferred dots – a combination denoting a slight staccato known as 'portato'. As early as 1785, however, he wrote dozens of staccato dots in the autograph of his piano quartets (WoO 36), clearly distinguishing them from the more common dashes (here slightly slanted). A few theorists of the time state that the dash represented a shorter staccato, and this was evidently Beethoven's understanding too. Thus right from the start of his career he was aware of a difference between the two symbols.

This notational distinction largely disappeared in his later manuscripts, but definite staccato dots do still appear occasionally, e.g. in Op. 26.I, where they seem clear and were printed as dots in the first edition. Unfortunately, Beethoven's publishers often treated his staccato marks very casually, changing some or all of his dashes into dots and making it impossible to identify genuine dots if no autograph survives. Not all his publishers were so cavalier, however. In Op. 31 No. 1.II the dots and dashes are printed fairly consistently, with dots occurring mainly on repeated notes and light scale patterns, where a more delicate attack seems appropriate (a similar distribution has been observed with Haydn and Mozart: see Rosenblum 1988, p. 186). Although the autograph is lost, the engraver clearly believed the two types of staccato mark were worth preserving.

Another element to consider is Beethoven's writing habits, for he tended to put more energy into writing staccatos where he wanted the pianist to put more energy into playing them, although this habit may have been largely subconscious. Thus his dashes can dwindle almost to dots in gentle passages but become quite long where a sharp attack is essential. Such subtleties (and inconsistencies) cannot be conveyed by any standard printed notation, but it is surely desirable to indicate something of his underlying intentions where possible. Accordingly, where a symbol is clear in the autograph it has normally been retained here; any resulting inconsistencies may represent places where Beethoven had in mind a sound between a very short and a longer staccato, and varied the notation without checking. Where the symbol is ambiguous, a dash has generally been used here, following his normal preference; but dots are used where they seem to reflect better his apparent intentions (e.g. in some light scale passages). Where there is no autograph, staccato signs have been standardized as his normal dashes, except in portato passages or where there is a clear pattern that suggests dots were intended. Always, however, the symbols are only rough guides and it is up to the performer to decide exactly how short to make each staccato, bearing its context in mind. Sometimes dots and dashes can be interpreted rather successfully as finger staccato and wrist (or arm) staccato respectively.

## Ornaments

The most common ornament in Beethoven's music is the trill, but its execution is problematic. Theorists in the 18th century indicated that trills began on the note above the written one, but by 1830 they were recommending trills to begin on the written note itself. Thus Beethoven lived at a time of transition from an upper-note to a main-note start. The only known occasion when he actually wrote out a recommended performance of one of his trills – in the finale of the 'Waldstein' Sonata (1803–4) – he used a main-note start, but then changed it to an upper-note start! In his earliest sonatas, modern performers should therefore begin trills on the upper note, but in later sonatas, either method is normally legitimate. Sometimes, however, an upper-note start is marked by a grace note and is therefore obligatory. On the other hand, a main-note start should always be used if the previous note is one step higher and is slurred to the trilled note, as is made clear, for instance, in Clementi's *Introduction* (1801; see Bibliographical References).

The end of the trill is also problematical. Some theorists indicated that trills should finish with a turn (also known as a suffix, termination or *Nachschlag*) even where none was written, but this was evidently not Beethoven's view, at least in his later years. When sending a correction list to London for his 'Hammerklavier' Sonata, he indicated certain places where a final turn to a trill had been wrongly omitted. Since his list addressed only important errors, he clearly regarded the presence or absence of a written turn to be significant. The implication, therefore, is that if he did not write one, none should be played. In earlier works, however, there may be a few places where he intended (or allowed) one but omitted to write it in.

In Beethoven's day, single grace notes were normally played not before the beat but on the beat, as were groups of two or three grace notes and also arpeggiandos. Single grace notes could be played either with almost no duration or as long appoggiaturas of half the value of the main note following. Both types were often notated in the same way by a small note, with the performer left to decide which interpretation was more appropriate. Some composers, however, including Beethoven, provided a clue to the intended duration by means of the precise note-length of each ornament. Debate still continues about exactly what Beethoven's note-lengths signify, but they apparently have specific meanings (see Cooper 2003). The evidence indicates that, where the written ornament is less than half the length of the main note (discounting any dots and ties), it was to be held for roughly its own value or less (i.e. almost no duration), with the main note taking up the rest of the time available. This normally occurs on rising figures. Where the written ornament is half, or more than half, the length of the main note, it was to be held for half the time available, with the main note taking up the other half, as generally recommended by theorists of the day. These long appoggiaturas normally occur on falling figures, and were given an expressive accent. In the present edition, suggestions for single grace-notes are based on these principles.

The modern convention of a crossed quaver for acciaccatura had not then evolved. This symbol was used by some scribes and engravers, however, in place of a semiquaver (similarly, a crossed semiquaver or double-crossed quaver could be used in place of a demisemiquaver). Beethoven himself never used this symbol, but some of his semiquaver ornaments were copied as crossed quavers by copyists and engravers who knew that this meant the same thing. Where the present edition is based on a source that uses this symbol, it has therefore been changed back to Beethoven's own notational form, i.e. a small semiquaver. To leave it as a crossed quaver would be misleading since this symbol now means something different.

Upper mordents appear occasionally, and should normally be played as a three-note figure beginning on the written note, with the first two notes as quick as possible. Thus they should be rhythmically the same as a double grace note, though in practice they usually appear on very quick notes, so that a triplet figure is almost unavoidable. In Beethoven's first three sonatas (1783), however, the mordent symbol probably often denotes a four-note ornament beginning on the upper note – a relic of the symbol's earlier meaning of trill-without-turn.

Less consistency is found with turns, which are sometimes placed above a note and sometimes slightly later. Where they are directly above, a four-note figure, beginning above the written note, is intended. If the turn is placed later than the note, the main note should be sounded first and the four-note turn tucked in shortly afterwards, but there is some flexibility over its exact rhythm, which depends partly on the metrical and expressive context and partly on the taste of the performer. The turn should normally be played rapidly, however, regardless of the speed of the surrounding music.

A few rare ornament signs are also encountered. For the present edition, editorial suggestions for these and other ornaments are placed above the stave where appropriate. A summary of the usual ornament signs and their recommended interpretation is given below:

All ornaments are to be played legato, and slurs have been added to some of the suggestions above the stave as a reminder of this. It must be emphasized that ornaments should be enjoyed by the performer for their decorative quality, rather than feared as a hazard, and a certain amount of tasteful flexibility is appropriate.

## Repeats

In an ideal performance all repeat marks should be observed. The notion that they are optional and were normally omitted is incorrect (though some performers certainly used to treat the printed text with considerable freedom). Beethoven thought long and hard about his repeat marks, occasionally cancelling them at the last minute, and so it is clear that he did not simply include them out of habit or convention. Even in the reprise of a minuet after a trio section, it seems that repeats should still be observed unless the score is marked otherwise, despite the modern convention of omitting them. Where necessity dictates, however, a repeat might be omitted without too much harm.

## Editorial Method

A single source of each sonata, normally the autograph score or first edition, has been used as the copy-text, and all deviations from it have been indicated, either on the page itself or in the Commentary to the individual sonata. As explained above, however, it often happens that no source consistently reflects Beethoven's intentions better than any other: a manuscript copy or the first printed edition may incorporate corrections and late revisions that are not in his autograph score, yet it might also include copying errors. Thus wherever the copy-text is believed to be inferior to another source, the readings from that source have been adopted as the main text. The aim has been to reproduce as closely as possible what are believed to be Beethoven's final intentions for the written text, even though these may not all be found in one source and are occasionally ambiguous. In parallel passages (such as an exposition and recapitulation) random minor discrepancies sometimes occur, e.g. in slurring, note lengths or occasionally an actual inconspicuous note. Beethoven seems not to have been bothered by such minutiae, and therefore nor should we: they have been allowed to stand as slight irregularities. Where one of the two versions seems positively faulty, however, it has been brought into line with the other, and the change noted. Distinguishing between minor variants and positive errors is a matter of editorial judgement, and not always clear-cut.

The edition matches the copy-text exactly apart from the following points:

a) Titles have been standardized, with the original titles noted in the Commentary. Certain performance instructions have also been standardized, e.g. *cres* as *cresc.*, *dol* as *dolce* and *ligato* as *legato*, as have turns printed upside down or with a qualifying accidental above instead of below the sign. Bar numbers have been added.

b) Redundant accidentals have normally been retained except on tied notes or notes repeated almost immediately. They can be useful as cautionary accidentals. Cautionary accidentals from secondary sources have also been incorporated in places. Any extra ones needed are shown in small type.

c) Editorial suggestions for certain ornaments are placed above the stave (see above for further explanations of ornament signs), and the old arpeggiando sign is modernized.

d) Minor notational changes have sometimes been made, provided the change could not affect the interpretation. For example, the clef, the direction of note stems (where it has no significance) and the distribution of notes between staves are occasionally altered for greater clarity. In general, however, the copy-text has been followed, even if the notation is slightly unconventional, since it could help explain the role and function of the notes. This principle applies also to the presence or absence of internal double bars, which have not been silently modernized.

e) Original beaming of quavers and semiquavers has been retained from the copy-text (except in the very rare places where it is positively misleading), but variants in beaming in other sources have not been noted. In some places the original beaming provides clues about articulation and phrasing, although elsewhere it may have no significance.

f) Beethoven's own fingerings appear in large type, similar in size to what was common in his day. They are supplemented by recommended editorial fingering by David Ward (in normal type), and by occasional suggestions for which hand to use, indicated by ⌈ (for left hand) or ⌊ (for right). But performers should work out for themselves what fingering best suits their own unique hands, and editorial fingering has been kept somewhat restricted so as not to clutter the page. None has been added in the last five sonatas: anyone capable of tackling these should be able to devise suitable fingerings, and may find editorial ones more intrusive than helpful.

g) Editorial ties and slurs, which are added only where their omission is believed to be an oversight, are marked thus: ⌒ Editorial extensions of existing ties and slurs are shown by broken lines. Where slurs are only fractionally short (i.e. by less than one note), however, they have been extended without indication. Slurs that are slightly too long have likewise been curtailed.

h) Other editorial additions, whether corrections or supplementary performance recommendations, are shown by means of small type or square brackets, and are generally kept to a minimum (restricted mainly to amplification based on directly parallel passages, clarifying uncertainties, and correcting apparently erroneous signs).

i) The distinction between staccato dots and dashes has been retained only where it appears significant or the autograph is unambiguous. Elsewhere dots, and symbols between dot and dash, have been replaced by dashes, except under slurs, where dots are retained and any dashes found in printed sources are replaced by dots.

j) Where dynamics are slightly misaligned in early editions, as often happens, they have been adjusted using common sense.

Where the misalignment is more substantial or uncertain, the amendment has been noted. Where Beethoven's autograph survives, the alignment of dynamics is carefully followed.

k) All other deviations from the copy-text are listed in the Commentary. Superior readings from secondary sources are incorporated and the fact noted. Other major variants in secondary sources are also indicated, but minor variants in secondary sources, including obvious misreadings and omissions, are generally not listed unless they are considered possibly significant.

The Commentary for each sonata, besides discussing textual and notational problems in the sources, also includes suggestions on matters of performance. A few of these (marked DFT and CCz repectively) are derived from Donald Tovey's notes in the Associated Board's old edition (London, 1931) or from Czerny 1970 (see References), and Czerny's suggested metronome marks are provided for each movement. It has not been felt desirable to include all of Tovey's comments, however, since many have been undermined by more recent research or reflect performing practices of the 1930s rather than of Beethoven's day. Nor does it seem appropriate to include suggestions by the numerous other writers who have addressed the subject of how to play Beethoven's sonatas. Instead, performers are encouraged to seek out some of this literature (in addition to items in the References below), such as books by Edwin Fischer, Charles Rosen, Richard Taub and, for those who read German, Joachim Kaiser and Jürgen Uhde, where much helpful advice may be read.

In the Commentary, abbreviations for notes are used as, for example: **31.rh.6** denotes the sixth symbol (note or rest) in the right-hand (i.e. upper) stave in bar 31. Individual voices may also be specified, namely **s** (soprano), **a** (alto), **t** (tenor), **b** (bass), **s2** (2nd soprano). Pitch: $CC$–$BB$, $C$–$B$, $c$–$b$, $c^1$–$b^1$, $c^2$–$b^2$, $c^3$–$b^3$, $c^4$–$b^4$; $c^1$ = middle C.

*Summary of Editorial Additions:*

Bar numbers

Crossed ties and slurs

Broken-line extensions to slurs

Small notes (other than grace notes), accidentals and other symbols

Everything within [ ]

All fingering except that shown in large type

⌈ or ⌊ indicating which hand to use

Supplementary staves recommending interpretation of ornament signs

## BIBLIOGRAPHICAL REFERENCES

Barth, George, *The Pianist as Orator: Beethoven and the Transformation of Keyboard Style*, Ithaca and London, 1992.

Brandenburg, Sieghard, ed., *Ludwig van Beethoven: Briefwechsel Gesamtausgabe*, 7 vols., Munich, 1996–8.

Clementi, Muzio, *Introduction to the Art of Playing on the Piano Forte*, London, 1801 (reprinted New York, 1974).

Cooper, Barry, 'Beethoven's Appoggiaturas: Long or Short?', *Early Music*, xxxi (2003), 165–78.

Czerny, Carl, *On the Proper Performance of All Beethoven's Works for the Piano*, ed. Paul Badura-Skoda, Vienna, 1970.

Jeffery, Brian, ed., *Ludwig van Beethoven: The 32 Piano Sonatas in reprints of the first and early editions*, London, 1989.

Newman, William S., *Beethoven on Beethoven: Playing His Piano Music His Way*, New York and London, 1988.

Rosenblum, Sandra P., *Performance Practices in Classic Piano Music*, Bloomington and Indianapolis, 1988.

Further literature is cited in the commentaries on the individual sonatas.

## ACKNOWLEDGEMENTS

Particular thanks are due first and foremost to David Ward, who has collaborated throughout this project with great diligence and efficiency. Besides furnishing these sonatas with often ingenious fingerings, he has commented with much perception on the entire edition and commentary as it took shape, and has made many valuable suggestions that have been incorporated into the text. The edition and commentary have also been scrutinized in detail by Clive Brown, who has made many further valuable suggestions for improvement. In addition I must thank all the staff of ABRSM Publishing, and in particular the director Leslie East, for their unfailing courtesy, helpfulness and encouragement. Other past or present members of staff who must be mentioned in this context include David Blackwell, Philip Croydon, Jonathan Lee and Caroline Perkins, while Andrew Jones has had the unenviable task of engraving the often unorthodox musical notation. Thanks are also due to several other individuals for their helpful comments, ideas or assistance, including Christine Brown, Hywel Davies, Jonathan Del Mar, William Drabkin, Richard Jones and Tong Peng. I owe an enormous debt of gratitude to all the libraries that have supplied me with photocopies or microfilms of source material, and in some cases given me direct access to the original sources: the Staatsbibliothek zu Berlin, Preussischer Kulturbesitz, Musikabteilung; the Beethoven-Archiv, Bonn; the Oddělení dějin hudby, Moravské zemské muzeum, Brno; the Fitzwilliam Museum, Cambridge; the Biblioteka Jagiellońska, Kraków; the British Library, London; the Bodleian Library, Oxford; the Stadtarchiv, Trier; the Gesellschaft der Musikfreunde, Vienna; the Österreichische Nationalbibliothek, Vienna; and the Library of Congress, Washington DC. The Arts and Humanities Research Council are to be thanked for providing a generous grant for research leave that enabled the rapid completion of the final stages of the research involved in the preparation of the edition. Finally I must express my deepest gratitude to my wife Susan, who has shown great interest in the progress of the edition and has provided all kinds of indirect support that have facilitated its progress and completion.

BARRY COOPER
Manchester, 2007

# NOTE ON EDITORIAL FINGERING

Czerny reports that he was instructed by his teacher Beethoven to read C.P.E. Bach's *Essay on the True Art of Playing Keyboard Instruments*, first published (in German) in 1753. This remarkably thorough book contains no fewer than 38 pages on fingering. Here are two extracts:

> there is only one good system of keyboard fingering, and very few passages permit alternative fingerings. Again, almost every new figure calls for its own distinctive fingering...

> correct employment of the fingers is inseparably related to the whole art of performance. More is lost through poor fingering than can be replaced by all conceivable artistry and good taste.

Some 35 years later a more flexible approach is shown in the *School of Clavier Playing* (the *Klavierschule*) by Daniel Gottlob Türk:

> There are passages where only one kind of fingering is possible and others which can be fingered in a number of ways....It would not be easy to find two keyboard players who...would make use of the same fingering throughout. Both are nevertheless able to play excellently and have good fingering

Then follow 58 pages on the subject, with examples of almost every type of passage and ways in which to finger them.

Suggestions for fingering can be helpful, particularly for the less experienced player and in a teaching edition such as this. But it is a curious exercise to make them when one is well aware that much of what is suggested may be replaced by a teacher's or student's preferred patterns. When adding fingerings to these extraordinary works I have considered the following points (among others):

a) Comfort of hand position, taking into account where the hand is coming from and going to. Also, the average size of hand and the differences between hands, e.g. the very variable stretch between inner fingers.
b) Dynamic requirements, e.g. using stronger fingers for louder, more emphasized notes.
c) Phrasing and articulation, how to help fingers and hands follow the phrasing, and not assuming a continuous legato.
d) Pedalling and, in the earlier sonatas especially, not assuming the use of pedal except in obviously resonant or arpeggiated passages. Fingers should be able to achieve a convincing legato without relying on pedalling.

After completing the fingering for the first edited sonata, I wrote the following to Barry Cooper:

> It has been a fascinating but also somewhat unsatisfactory task, as I know that much of what I find works for me will not be so comfortable for different hands and will inevitably be changed....I have left some passages and particularly chords and ornaments without much, if any, fingering, as so much depends on the shape and size of the hand for chords and on general facility for ornaments. Sometimes I wondered if there was any point in putting in any fingering at all; and I think some of the fingerings may be surprising or at best idiosyncratic. Also, how much to put in? There are times when you have to put in a lot to make the patterns clear. I have little hesitation in taking 'right hand' notes with the left hand, or vice versa, if this seems a more comfortable solution. However, I know that some people feel very strongly that this should never be done. I feel that piano music is written for ten fingers, more than for two hands – although there are times when a composer wants a special effect by employing the hands in a particular way. I also favour substitution and fingers crossing over each other when required.

As part of the process, Barry Cooper queried my more unusual fingerings and as a result some were revised or simply left out. If 'surprising' fingerings remain, these must be held to be my responsibility. All passages were tried out on my Viennese fortepianos as well as on modern instruments.

To conclude, here is C.P.E. Bach again, describing what must be the aim of good fingering – to be able to forget about it and concentrate on the music:

> through diligent practice, execution becomes, and must become, so mechanical that a stage is reached when, without further concern, full attention may be directed to the expression of more important matters.

DAVID WARD
London, 2007

# EINFÜHRUNG

## EDITORISCHE PRINZIPIEN UND QUELLEN

Beethoven hat im Lauf seines Lebens 35 Klaviersonaten veröffentlicht. Sie umspannen fast seine ganze Laufbahn, von den drei Sonaten, die 1783 herauskamen, als er zwölf Jahre alt war, bis zur großartigen c-Moll-Sonate op. 111 von 1822. Sie sind bis heute einzigartig und bilden einen Eckstein des pianistischen Repertoires. In zahlreichen Editionen wurden sie veröffentlicht, aber in den meisten der älteren wurden nur wenige Versuche unternommen, Beethovens Absichten genau wiederzugeben. Die Herausgeber haben den gedruckten Text oft geändert, um ihn dem Geschmack und der Aufführungspraxis ihrer Zeit anzupassen (obwohl die Noten selbst kaum je geändert wurden). Heute hingegen hat sich die Auffassung durchgesetzt, dass Beethovens Klaviersonaten (wie andere Musik vergangener Jahrhunderte) am besten so aufgeführt werden sollten, wie es der Komponist – soweit wir dies wissen – damals im Auge hatte, nicht in einer verzerrten, durch spätere Aufführungspraktiken beeinflussten Form. Anderenfalls würde man etwas anderes spielen als eine „Sonate von Beethoven"; es wäre vielmehr eine Beethoven-Sonate in der Bearbeitung eines Dritten, sei es nun der Herausgeber, der Bearbeiter oder der Interpret. Sogar geringfügige Abweichungen, die nachweisbar den ursprünglichen Intentionen widersprechen, unterscheiden sich nicht prinzipiell, sondern nur graduell von sehr freizügigen Bearbeitungen. Obwohl solche Bearbeitungen ihre eigenen Verdienste haben mögen, können sie nicht länger als Sonaten von Beethoven gelten – die Reinheit der Komposition wurde beschädigt. Es ist sogar höchst unwahrscheinlich, dass solche Revisionen Beethovens Ideen verbessern; das Ergebnis wäre mit einiger Sicherheit nicht nur anders, sondern auch schlechter.

Das heißt nicht, dass es für jede Sonate nur eine einzige korrekte Aufführungsweise gibt. Denn die Musik erlaubt viele Interpretationen, und es ist notwendig, dass die Pianisten einiges von ihren eigenen Gefühlen und Persönlichkeitsmerkmalen in ihre Aufführungen einbringen. Nicht einmal Beethoven hat während seines Lebens nur ein einziges, unverändertes Interpretationsideal beibehalten. Dennoch sollte man unter keinen Umständen Aufführungselemente einführen, von denen man weiß, dass sie seinen Intentionen und Erwartungen direkt zuwiderlaufen, selbst wenn diese Intentionen gewisse Freiheiten des Zugangs erlauben.

Die vorliegende Edition nimmt solche Prinzipien als Ausgangspunkt. Sie möchte in erster Linie den musikalischen Text genau so präsentieren (so weit dies möglich ist), wie ihn Beethoven sich vorgestellt hat, was die genaue Prüfung aller relevanten Quellen voraussetzt, und zweitens möchte sie die Bedeutung seiner Notation ausreichend erläutern; denn abweichend von der üblichen Meinung hat sich die Notation seit 1800 beträchtlich weiterentwickelt, und bestimmte ungeschriebene Gesetze der damaligen Zeit müssen heute explizit genannt werden. Alle 35 Sonaten sind enthalten (die meisten anderen Editionen lassen ohne Begründung die ersten drei aus) und sie werden in der chronologischen Folge ihrer Entstehung vorgestellt, so dass die Entwicklung von Beethovens Stil leichter erkannt werden kann. (Es gibt nur zwei kleine Ausnahmen: op. 49 Nr. 1 und 2 werden zusammen in der numerischen Reihenfolge vor op. 7 präsentiert, obwohl die Nr. 1 offenbar nach Nr. 2 komponiert wurde, wahrscheinlich auch nach op. 7; und op. 78 erscheint vor op. 79, obwohl es wahrscheinlich direkt danach entstand.)

Wenn sie eine moderne Edition älterer Musik benutzen, sollten die Pianisten sich der Geschichte hinter den ihnen sichtbaren Noten bewusst werden. Bei Beethovens Sonaten wurden die Noten, die in seinem Kopf entstanden, oft in verschiedenen Formen auf dem Klavier ausprobiert, bevor er sie niederschrieb. Er machte auch zahlreiche rohe Entwürfe in Form von Skizzen, bevor die endgültige Niederschrift – das **Autograph** – aufgeschrieben wurde. Einzelne Details wurden dann auf verschiedene Weise revidiert. Danach fertigte ein professioneller Kopist normalerweise eine **Reinschrift** an, welche von Beethoven überprüft und korrigiert wurde, manchmal mit einigen weiteren Berichtigungen. Die Reinschrift (oder das Autograph selbst) wurde dann zum Drucker geschickt, der eine Reihe von Druckplatten stach und einen Korrekturabzug herstellte. Dieser wurde im allgemeinen Beethoven zur Überprüfung zugeschickt, bevor dann eine Serie von etwa 100 korrigierten Exemplaren gedruckt wurde – der **Erstdruck**. Wenn weitere Fehler bemerkt wurden, konnten zusätzliche Korrekturen vorgenommen werden, die dann zu einem zweiten oder vielleicht sogar dritten Druck führten. Daraus folgt, dass keine dieser Quellen eine endgültige Version enthält. Das Autograph kann Notationsfehler enthalten – beispielsweise vergaß Beethoven manchmal ein wichtiges Vorzeichen – und in ihm fehlen alle noch in letzter Minute vorgenommenen Eintragungen in die Abschrift des Kopisten. Aber selbst wenn diese Abschrift diese Eintragungen und die vorher fehlenden Vorzeichen enthält, kann sie Abschreibefehler enthalten, die von Beethoven übersehen wurden. Das gilt auch für die gedruckte Ausgabe, vor allem dann, wenn Beethoven keine Gelegenheit zur Überprüfung hatte. Es ist deshalb irreführend, wenn einige moderne Editionen sich als Urtext-Ausgaben bezeichnen, denn wahrscheinlich gab es nie einen völlig fehlerfreien Originaltext.

Bei bestimmten Sonaten entstehen Probleme durch eine spätere Edition, die von einem anderen Verleger in Zusammenarbeit mit Beethoven selbständig gestochen und herausgegeben wurde und die teilweise leicht abweichende Lesarten enthält. Außerdem muss bei den meisten Sonaten wenigstens eine Quelle – das Autograph oder die Kopisten-Reinschrift – heute als verloren gelten; tatsächlich existiert für viele Sonaten, vor allem für die frühen, nur noch die Originalausgabe, welche beträchtliche Fehler enthalten kann. Das Konzept einer „Originalausgabe" ist ebenfalls belastet von Problemen, die von modernen Herausgebern nicht immer erkannt werden. Einzelne Kopien oder **Exemplare** mögen noch vom Erstdruck herrühren, aber einige andere, auf den ersten Blick identisch aussehende, können einem leicht modifizierten späteren Druck entstammen. Andere können von einer späteren **Auflage** herrühren, wenn der gleiche

Druckplatten-Satz von einem anderen Verleger verwendet wurde; nur wenn ein neuer Druckplatten-Satz verwendet wird, entweder durch den gleichen oder häufiger durch einen anderen Verleger, darf man dies als eine spätere **Ausgabe** bezeichnen.

Die meisten dieser anderen frühen Ausgaben, von denen es viele gibt, wurden einfach aus bereits existierenden Editionen kopiert. Sie bringen stets neue Fehler, während sie im allgemeinen nur einige offensichtliche Fehler korrigieren. Man kann in der Regel annehmen, dass die Verleger wegen ihrer Veröffentlichung keinen direkten Kontakt zu Beethoven aufnahmen, und so sind diese unterschiedlichen Lesarten nicht autorisiert. Entsprechend blieben alle diese Ausgaben für unsere Zwecke unberücksichtigt, es sei denn, ein direkter Kontakt Beethovens mit diesen Verlegern kann eindeutig nachgewiesen werden. Bei Ausgaben, an denen er aber beteiligt war, sollte ein moderner Herausgeber im Idealfall alle bekannten Exemplare berücksichtigen, falls eine wichtige und authentische Abweichung vorliegt. Dies war bei der vorliegenden Ausgabe nicht möglich, und es hätte wohl auch kaum den endgültigen Text beeinflusst; aber wenigstens zwei Exemplare wurden normalerweise geprüft – die aus Brian Jefferys Faksimile-Ausgabe (s. die Literaturhinweise unten) und mindestens eine weitere – also nicht nur eine einzige Vorlage. ( Jefferys Faksimili wurden übrigens während der Reproduktion gereinigt und zufällige Flecken entfernt. Unglücklicherweise verschwanden dabei einige Staccato-Punkte etc., was gelegentlich kleinere Abweichungen von der Originalausgabe verursachte.)

Wo Beethoven in einem sehr späten Stadium absichtliche Änderungen vornahm, ist das meist die letzte Version – die Fassung letzter Hand –, die als die gültige betrachtet wird. Manchmal ist es allerdings unklar, ob die Änderungen in letzter Minute als Flüchtigkeit zu bewerten sind oder als bewusste Verbesserungsversuche. Jede moderne Ausgabe braucht deshalb an solchen Stellen ein gewisses Maß editorischer Spekulation. Die vorliegende Ausgabe enthält die Lesarten, die als sein letzter Wille angesehen werden können (so weit dies festzustellen ist), während der Kommentar die Stellen benennt, wo es begründete Zweifel gibt. Es wäre unpraktikabel, eine ausführliche Begründung für jeden editorischen Schritt zu geben, aber jede Entscheidung ist das Ergebnis sorgfältiger Untersuchung der stilistischen wie textlichen Faktoren und versucht, der Abwägung der Möglichkeiten Rechnung zu tragen. Wo eine Unklarheit existiert, das muss betont werden, betrifft das fast immer kleinere Details wie die Länge oder Existenz von Legatobögen und Crescendo-Zeichen; nur selten werden die tatsächlichen Noten in Frage gestellt.

## Aufführungspraxis

Einen korrekten musikalischen Text durch sorgfältiges Quellenstudium zu erhalten, ist ein unentbehrlicher erster Schritt zur Aufführung einer Beethoven-Sonate. Aber sogar wenn jedes Notendetail auf dem Klavier genau wiedergegeben wird, garantiert das noch keine zufriedenstellende Aufführung. Zu Lebzeiten des Komponisten gab es außerdem viele ungeschriebene Gesetze, die bei jeder Aufführung beachtet werden mussten. Einige davon sind noch heute gebräuchlich, während andere wieder erlernt werden müssen. Diese zweite Kategorie war gerade in den letzten Jahren Gegenstand vieler Forschungen und die Literatur zu diesem Thema ist inzwischen recht umfangreich. Besonders bemerkenswert sind die Bücher von William S. Newman und Sandra P. Rosenblum (s. die Literaturhinweise unten), denen sich der Leser zuwenden soll, wenn er sich detaillierter über die hier diskutierten Probleme informieren möchte. Einige Aufführungsfragen sind allerdings noch umstritten und werden wahrscheinlich nie eindeutig beantwortet werden können. In der vorliegenden Ausgabe gehören zu jeder Sonate ausführliche editorische Bemerkungen, die begründete Ratschläge zu vielen problematischen Passagen bieten, wo entweder der Notentext oder seine Interpretation in irgendeiner Weise mehrdeutig ist. Diese Hinweise enthalten notwendigerweise ein subjektives Element, und die Interpreten haben das Recht, die Meinungen des Herausgebers zu übergehen, wenn sie dafür hinreichende Gründe haben.

### Instrumente

Als Beethoven seine frühesten Klaviersonaten in den 1780ern und 90ern veröffentlichte, unterschieden sich die Instrumente, für die er schrieb, beträchtlich vom modernen Klavier – so sehr, dass man sie heute manchmal als Fortepianos bezeichnet, um den Unterschied hervorzuheben. Sie hatten einen leiseren Ton und einen leichteren Anschlag, der Klang verschwand viel rascher, die Dämpfungsaufhebung (soweit vorhanden) schuf weniger Resonanz, es gab mehr Unterschiede zwischen den Registern, und der Tonumfang umfasste nur fünf Oktaven ($F1$ bis $f^3$). Es ist tatsächlich nicht notwendig, ein Fortepiano zu benutzen, um die frühen Sonaten wirkungsvoll zu spielen. Denn es gab große klangliche Unterschiede zwischen den einzelnen Klavieren; dennoch hat Beethoven keinen Instrumententyp als völlig ungeeignet für seine Musik abgelehnt (noch hat er jemals einen gefunden, der ihn ganz zufrieden stellte). Dennoch sollten die Pianisten sich mit der Klanglichkeit der frühen Klaviere vertraut machen, entweder durch Aufnahmen oder, besser noch, durch direkten Zugang. Solche Instrumente, die viele schöne und auffallende Eigenschaften besitzen, die spätere Hersteller eher glätteten, geben tiefe Einblicke in die Art der Klangwelt, die Beethoven sich für seine Sonaten vorstellte. Diese Klangeigenschaften können dann bis zu einem gewissen Maße auf einem modernen Instrument wiedergegeben werden.

Zu Beethovens Lebzeiten haben die Klavierbauer ständig versucht, ihre Instrumente größer und lauter zu machen. In den 1820er Jahren besaßen viele schon einen Tonumfang von sechseinhalb Oktaven, und Modifikationen wie dickere Saiten, stärkere Rahmen und größere Hämmer ließen sie schon viel ähnlicher heutigen Instrumenten klingen; aber in Ton und Anschlag unterscheiden sie sich immer noch beträchtlich von modernen Flügeln oder Klavieren. Die Tonhöhe der Instrumente war meist etwas tiefer als heute. Diese wurde aber nicht absolut festgelegt und der Unterschied betrug meist weniger als einen Halbton, so dass der moderne Kammerton ($a^1$ = 440) absolut akzeptabel ist. Die gleichschwebende Temperatur war kein festes Gesetz, aber etwas Ähnliches war üblich, was schnelle enharmonische Modulationen in entfernte Tonarten ermöglichte, während jede Ungleichmäßigkeit die Individualität jeder Tonart noch vergrößerte.

## Pedalisierung

Beethoven bezeichnet nur selten eine Pedalisierung und gar keine in den frühen Sonaten. Aber sein Schüler Carl Czerny berichtet uns, dass Beethoven die Pedale weitaus öfter verwendete, als es angezeigt ist (Czerny 1963, S. 22). Deshalb sollten moderne Interpreten nicht zögern, das rechte Pedal auch dort zu verwenden, wo es keine Angaben gibt, besonders in den späten Sonaten (der Pedalgebrauch steigerte sich wahrscheinlich zu Beethovens Lebzeiten beträchtlich, und die Haltewirkung wurde immer deutlicher). Andererseits sollte man der Versuchung widerstehen, es zu extensiv zu verwenden, um die Musik nicht in die Brühe eines fast allgegenwärtigen Hintergrundklangs einzutauchen. Es ist tatsächlich möglich, die frühen Sonaten (wenigstens bis opus 10 inklusive) ohne jeden Pedalgebrauch überzeugend zu spielen, und es ist lehrreich, dies einmal auszuprobieren, weil der Spieler dann gezwungen wird, tiefer über Fragen der Phrasierung, der Artikulation und der Fingersätze nachzudenken. Wo Beethoven eine Pedalisierung eingetragen hat, entweder mit dem rechten Pedal oder dem Dämpfungspedal, sollte das manchmal einen ungewöhnlichen Effekt erzeugen. Diese Effekte werden detailliert in den Kommentaren zu den betreffenden Sonaten behandelt.

## Tempo und Metronom

Vor der Erfindung des Metronoms konnte kein Komponist ein Tempo zuverlässig angeben. Man konnte Hinweise geben durch Begriffe wie *allegro* und *andante*, und auch durch die Wahl der Taktvorschrift **C** oder **¢** (das letztere bezeichnete ein schnelleres Tempo), aber vieles blieb dem Zufall überlassen, wie Beethoven selbst in einem Brief von 1812 beklagte. Kurz danach wurde jedoch das Metronom erfunden, und er war der erste bedeutende Komponist, der es benutzte. Nur bei einer einzigen seiner Sonaten – der „Hammerklavier"-Sonate op. 106 – hat er Metronomisierungen verwendet, und diese sind ziemlich schnell (Donald Tovey beschreibt sie für den ersten Satz als „unmöglich"). Viele seiner Metronom-Eintragungen bei seinen Quartetten und Symphonien sind aber ebenfalls eher schnell, und obwohl einige wenige ganz offensichtlich falsch sind, scheinen die anderen nur deshalb schnell zu sein, weil die Tempi in der Musik ganz allgemein in den Dekaden nach seinem Tod dazu tendierten, langsamer zu werden, so dass die Leute sich daran gewöhnten, vieles seiner Musik in einem etwas langsameren Puls zu hören, als er es sowohl in schnellen wie auch in langsamen Sätzen intendiert hatte.

Wo Beethovens eigene Metronomisierungen fehlen, können wir uns am besten an den Ratschlägen seines Schülers Czerny orientieren, der viele der Sonaten mit Beethoven selbst erarbeitet und später aus der Erinnerung Tempoempfehlungen niedergeschrieben hat. Einige davon wirken ebenfalls als recht schnell und bestätigen damit indirekt, dass Beethovens Angaben nicht auf einem Irrtum beruhten. (Es ist interessant, dass Czerny beim ersten Satz der „Hammerklavier"-Sonate das von Beethoven angegebene Tempo nicht als unmöglich ansieht, sondern nur als Ursache für „Schwierigkeiten" und die Notwendigkeit „aufmerksamer Übung": s. Czerny 1963, S. 66/58.) Czernys Metronomangaben werden hier in den Kommentaren wiedergegeben, aber in vielen Sätzen machte er bei unterschiedlichen Gelegenheiten unterschiedliche Angaben (Rosenblum 1988, S. 329–30, 355–61); in solchen Fällen wird die schnellste wie auch die langsamste Variante wiedergegeben (wenn nicht anders vermerkt). Es sei aber darauf hingewiesen, dass dies nur einen groben Rahmen angibt, der anderen Faktoren wie Raumakustik, der Qualität des Instruments und der Fähigkeit des Spielers noch angepasst werden kann. Außerdem sollten Metronomisierungen während eines Satzes nicht streng durchgehalten werden – sie bezeichnen nur das Anfangstempo. Es gibt zahlreiche Zeugnisse von Czerny und anderen, dass Flexibilität gestattet war, obwohl Beethoven von den Pianisten im Prinzip ein genaues Tempo erwartete, und es gibt viele Zusammenhänge, in denen die Musik zeitweise verlangsamt oder auch (seltener) beschleunigt werden kann. Zu den Passagen, in denen Czerny ein ritardando empfiehlt, gehören solche kurz vor der Wiederkehr des Hauptthemas, vor einer Fermate, vor einem neuen Tempo, und bei zarten Kadenzen (s. Barth 1992, vor allem S. 74–7, 85–6). Ein flexibles Tempo oder „rubato" kann bei ganzen Phrasen oder Abschnitten, Tongruppen oder auch nur bei einzelnen Noten oder Akkorden angewendet werden. Es sollte natürlich immer zur Verstärkung des Ausdrucks eingesetzt werden, nicht einfach als willkürliche Tempoveränderung. Das gleiche gilt für andere ungeschriebene Praktiken, die zu Beethovens Lebzeiten üblich waren, so das Spiel der rechten Hand kurz nach der linken Hand bei kantablen Melodien, und hinzufügende Arpeggien bei langsamen Akkorden.

## Dynamik

Da Beethovens Klaviere beträchtlich leiser waren als die modernen Instrumente, gab es weniger Möglichkeiten der Klangabstufung und weniger dynamische Ebenen konnten erkannt werden. Die Sonaten verwenden nur vier Grundstufen – $\boldsymbol{pp}$, $\boldsymbol{p}$, $\boldsymbol{f}$ und $\boldsymbol{ff}$ – sowie verschiedene Kombinationen wie $\boldsymbol{sf}$, $\boldsymbol{fp}$ und *cresc.*; dadurch ist der Unterschied zwischen $\boldsymbol{p}$ und $\boldsymbol{f}$ geringer als bei späterer Musik der Fall sein würde, wo oft $\boldsymbol{mp}$ und $\boldsymbol{mf}$ verwendet wird. Das Zeichen $\boldsymbol{f}$ erscheint gelegentlich als eine etwas weniger emphatische Alternative zu $\boldsymbol{sf}$, aber diese Bedeutung wird im allgemeinen aus dem Zusammenhang klar. Die erste Sonate mit einem $\boldsymbol{ppp}$ ist op. 7, aber dieses Zeichen bleibt sehr selten, während $\boldsymbol{mf}$ (s. op. 101) und $\boldsymbol{mp}$ (s. op. 111, wo es als „mezzo piano" ausgeschrieben wird) sogar noch seltener sind. Der Ausdruck *mezza voce* taucht auch gelegentlich auf und entspricht etwa $\boldsymbol{mp}$ oder $\boldsymbol{p}$. Das Zeichen $\boldsymbol{sfp}$ bezeichnet einen Akzent, dem sogleich ein $\boldsymbol{p}$ folgt; aber wo der Zusammenhang schon leise ist, sollte der Akzent selbst wahrscheinlich schwächer sein als ein wirkliches *sf*. Ebenfalls verwendet wird die Bezeichnung *rinforzando* oder *rinf.*, was soviel bedeutet wie „verstärkend" oder „anwachsend". Obwohl sich die Theoretiker nicht ganz einig waren über ihre Verwendung, hat Beethoven sie offenbar als eine mildere Form des *sf* angesehen; er benutzte sie meist nur bei einer einzigen Note oder einem Akkord, gelegentlich auch bei längeren Gebilden. Crescendo und diminuendo werden manchmal als Schwellzeichen notiert. Das Diminuendo-Zeichen folgt oft einem *sf* oder einer anderen lauten Dynamik-Bezeichnung. Wo es aber alleine steht, entweder auf einer einzigen Note oder auf mehrere erweitert, scheint es einen Akzent zu bezeichnen (weniger stark als *sf*, da es zusammen mit diesem verwendet werden kann), gefolgt von einem Abschwellen zur vorangehenden dynamischen Ebene.

## Legatobögen und Artikulation

Bei der Betrachtung von Beethovens Legatobögen muss man sich daran erinnern, dass im 18. Jahrhundert der etwas gestoßene Anschlag die Norm darstellte. Beispielsweise stellte Daniel Gottlob Türk 1789 fest: „Bey den Tönen, welche auf die gewöhnliche Art d. h. weder gestossen noch geschleift, vorgetragen werden sollen, hebt man den Finger ein wenig früher, als es die Dauer der Note erfordert, von den Tasten" (*Klavierschule*, S. 356). Indem man den Moment, an dem der Finger angehoben wird, von einer Art staccato bis fast zum legato variierte, konnte eine große Feinheit der Artikulation und des Ausdrucks erzielt werden. Wenn der Komponist eine dichte legato-Verbindung von einer Note zur nächsten wünschte, zeigte er dies durch einen kurzen Legatobogen an; wenn eine ganze Passage legato gespielt werden sollte, verwendete er einen langen Legatobogen, heute oft fälschlich als „Phrasierungsbogen" bezeichnet – ein anachronistisches Konzept. Beethoven benutzte diese langen Legatobögen viel öfter als seine Vorgänger, aber es gibt auch Stellen, wo es überhaupt kein Artikulationszeichen gibt. Hier sollte dann ein etwas gestoßener Anschlag in der bei Türk beschriebenen Art verwendet werden, wenn es nicht gute Gründe für eine andere Spielweise gibt (beispielsweise, wenn eine ähnliche Passage direkt vorher mit Legatobögen versehen war). Diese Regel muss nicht unbedingt für Beethovens späte Werke gelten, weil zu dieser Zeit der Legatoanschlag mehr und mehr zur Norm wurde.

Türk führt auch an, dass die erste Note unter einem Legatobogen „sehr gelinde (kaum merklich) accentuiert" werden sollte (*Klavierschule*, S. 355). Diese Empfehlung gilt vor allem für kurze Bögen über zwei oder drei Noten, sollte aber auch bei längeren Bögen Berücksichtigung finden, weil sie auch dort oft passend ist. Hinsichtlich der letzten Note unter einem Bogen ist es nicht immer eindeutig, wie sie mit der nächsten Note verbunden werden soll. Die Situation wird nicht viel klarer durch Beethovens Bemerkung gegenüber Karl Holz vom August 1825: „Es ist nicht gleichgültig ob so ![Notenbeispiel] oder so ![Notenbeispiel] " (Brandenburg Hg., 1996–8, Nr. 2032). Beethoven bezieht sich hier auf Streichermusik, wo der Unterschied zwischen beiden Fällen ganz eindeutig ist, weil er das Bogenspiel beeinflusst. Bei Klaviermusik ist der Unterschied viel weniger offensichtlich,

sollte aber dennoch beachtet werden. Das wird deutlich, wenn man Ausschnitte aus zwei seiner Sonaten vergleicht:

op. 14 Nr. 2.III

op. 49 Nr. 2.II

Im ersten Fall stellt jede Dreitongruppe eine einzelne Geste dar, die legato zu spielen ist, auf der dritten Note schwächer werdend. Dagegen sollten beim zweiten Fall die Staccato-Noten wohl etwas mehr betont werden als im ersten Beispiel; sie sollten auch leicht abgetrennt werden von der vorangehenden Note, wenn das Tempo des Stückes und die Klaviermechanik das zulassen.

Bei kurzen Legatobögen über nur zwei, drei oder manchmal auch vier Noten sollte die letzte Note der Gruppe gekürzt werden. Deshalb sollte beim folgenden Beispiel die zweite Note jedes Paares staccato-ähnlich gespielt werden, wobei es gleichgültig ist, ob eine wiederholte Note folgt oder nicht. Sie kann auch leicht verfrüht angeschlagen werden:

op. 31 Nr. 2.I

Bei längeren Bögen muss allerdings die letzte Note nicht vom Folgenden abgesetzt werden. Es war meist unbequem, sehr lange Legatobögen einzutragen, denn entweder verloren sie ihre Form oder störten das darüber- oder darunterliegende Notensystem; deshalb wurden sie gewöhnlich in kürzere Bögen unterteilt. Wie Czerny bemerkte, „Wenn kleinere Schleifbögen über 2 oder 3 Noten abgetheilt stehen, so wird die zweite oder dritte Note etwas abgestossen … Wenn aber Schleifbögen über mehreren Noten, obgleich abgetheilt, stehen, so wird angenommen, als ob es nur ein einziger wäre, und es darf kein Absetzen merkbar werden" (Czerny, *Pianoforte-Schule*, Bd. 1, S. 142–3). Deshalb sollten, wenn Czernys Hinweis gilt (obwohl er viele Jahre nach Beethovens frühen Sonaten niedergeschrieben wurde), zwei oder mehr benachbarte Bögen über mehr als zwei oder drei Noten jeweils wie ein durchgehender Legatobogen gespielt werden. In diesem Fall reduzieren sich unterschiedliche Bogensetzungen bei Exposition und Reprise zu bloßen Notationsvarianten. Die vorliegende Ausgabe behält dennoch die originalen Legatobögen bei, um solche Unregelmäßigkeiten anzuzeigen und um den Pianisten die Entscheidung zu lassen, ob bestimmte Unterbrechungen der Bögen für den Interpreten eine Bedeutung haben. Sie übernimmt auch alle irregulären Balkensetzungen bei Achtel- und Sechzehntelnoten aus dem Original, da diese möglicherweise subtile Aufschlüsse darüber geben, wie Beethoven bestimmte Notengruppen aufgefasst hat.

## Staccato

Das Hauptproblem mit Beethovens Staccati entspringt seiner gleichzeitigen Verwendung von Punkten und Strichen. In seinem oben zitierten Brief aus dem Jahre 1825 belehrte er seinen Kopisten, „wo ‥ über der Note darf kein ׀ ׀ statt dessen stehen u. so umgekehrt". Seine Notenautographe sind dennoch nicht immer eindeutig. Normalerweise verwendete er vertikale Striche, aber diese können so kurz sein, dass sie Punkten ähneln, wodurch offenkundige Abweichungen bei parallelen Passagen entstehen. Einige heutige Fachleute meinen deshalb, alle seine Staccato-Zeichen sollten eigentlich Striche sein; Ausnahmen seien nur diejenigen unter Legatobögen, wo er offenbar immer Punkte bevorzugte – eine Kombination, die ein leichtes Staccato, auch „portato" genannt, bezeichnet. Aber schon 1785 schrieb er Dutzende von Staccato-Punkten im Autograph seiner Klavierquartette (WoO 36), die er klar unterschied von den häufiger verwendeten Strichen (hier leicht schräg gestellt). Einige zeitgenössische Theoretiker schreiben, dass der Strich ein kürzeres Staccato bezeichnete, und so hat es offenbar auch Beethoven verstanden. Deshalb war ihm seit dem Beginn seiner Laufbahn die unterschiedliche Bedeutung beider Zeichen bewusst.

Diese Notations-Unterscheidung verschwand weitgehend in seinen späteren Manuskripten, aber deutliche Staccato-Punkte kehren gelegentlich immer noch wieder, so etwa in op. 26.I, wo sie eindeutig zu sein scheinen und in der Erstausgabe als Punkte gedruckt wurden. Unglücklicherweise haben Beethovens Verleger seine Staccato-Zeichen oft sehr salopp behandelt, indem sie einige oder alle seiner Striche in Punkte verwandelten und es so unmöglich machten, wirkliche Punkte zu identifizieren, wenn kein Autograph mehr vorhanden ist. Aber nicht alle seine Verleger waren so leichtfertig. In op. 31, Nr. 1.II sind die Punkte und Striche recht konsequent gedruckt, mit Punkten meist über wiederholten Noten und leichten Tonleiterausschnitten, wo ein eher delikater Anschlag angemessen erscheint (eine ähnliche Aufteilung wurde bei Haydn und Mozart bemerkt: s. Rosenblum 1988, S. 186). Obwohl das Autograph verloren ging, hat der Notenstecher es offenbar für wichtig gehalten, beide Arten der Staccato-Notation zu bewahren.

Zu berücksichtigen sind aber auch Beethovens Schreibgewohnheiten, denn üblicher Weise – allerdings wohl eher unterbewusst – schrieb er Staccati dann mit mehr Energie, wenn der Pianist sie mit mehr Energie spielen sollte. So können seine Striche bei zarten Passagen fast zu Punkten schrumpfen oder aber recht lang werden, wo ein scharfer Zugriff notwendig ist. Solche Feinheiten (oder Unregelmäßigkeiten) können von einer standardisierten Druckausgabe nicht vermittelt werden, aber es ist sicher wünschenswert, etwas von den zugrundeliegenden Absichten wiederzugeben, sofern dies möglich ist. Entsprechend wurden aus dem Autograph eindeutige Symbole in der Regel in dieser Ausgabe übernommen; sofern sich dadurch Unregelmäßigkeiten ergeben, stehen sie möglicherweise für Stellen, wo Beethoven sich einen Klang zwischen einem sehr kurzen und einem längeren Staccato vorstellte und die Notation ohne weitere Überprüfung änderte. Bei unklaren Zeichen wurde hier im allgemeinen, seiner normalen Praxis folgend, ein Strich

verwendet; hingegen werden Punkte eingesetzt, wo sie seine offensichtlichen Intentionen besser wiedergeben (z.B. in einigen leichten Tonleiterausschnitten). Wo ein Autograph fehlt, wurden Staccato-Zeichen an seine normalen Striche angepasst, mit Ausnahme von portato-Passagen oder wo eine klare Struktur nahe legt, dass Punkte gemeint waren. Immer jedoch geben diese Zeichen nur grobe Hinweise und es bleibt dem Ausführenden überlassen, wie kurz er jedes Staccato machen will, wenn er den Zusammenhang berücksichtigt. Manchmal empfiehlt es sich, Punkte und Striche als Finger-Staccato bzw. Hand-(oder Arm-)Staccato aufzufassen.

## Verzierungen

Die gebräuchlichste Verzierung in Beethovens Musik ist der Triller, wobei die Art der Ausführung umstritten ist. Die Theoretiker des 18. Jahrhunderts gaben an, dass Triller auf dem Ton über der geschriebenen Note begannen. Ab 1830 allerdings empfahlen sie, Triller auf der geschriebenen Note selbst zu beginnen. Beethoven lebte also in einer Übergangszeit zwischen dem Beginn auf der oberen Nebennote und dem auf der Hauptnote. Bei der einzigen bekannten Gelegenheit, wo er tatsächlich die gewünschte Aufführungsweise eines Trillers ausschrieb – im Finale seiner „Waldstein"-Sonate (1803–4) –, verwendete er einen Hauptnoten-Beginn, den er dann aber zum Nebennoten-Beginn änderte! In seinen frühesten Sonaten sollten heutige Interpreten deshalb Triller auf der oberen Nebennote beginnen, während in den späten Sonaten meist beide Methoden legitim sind. Manchmal allerdings wird der Beginn auf der oberen Nebennote durch eine Vorschlagsnote angegeben und ist dann zwingend. Andererseits sollte ein Hauptnoten-Beginn immer dann verwendet werden, wenn die vorangehende Note eine Stufe höher liegt und an die Trillernote angebunden wird, wie dies beispielsweise in Clementis *Introduction* erläutert wird (1801; s. Literaturhinweise).

Das Ende des Trillers ist ebenfalls problematisch. Einige Theoretiker gaben an, dass Triller auch da mit einem Doppelschlag enden sollten (auch bekannt als Endung oder Nachschlag), wo ein solcher nicht notiert war. Aber das entsprach offenbar nicht Beethovens Position, zumindest nicht in seinen späten Jahren. Als er eine Korrekturliste für seine „Hammerklavier"-Sonate nach London sandte, gab er bestimmte Stellen an, wo ein Triller-Nachschlag fälschlich weggelassen worden war. Da seine Liste nur wichtige Fehler enthielt, betrachtete er das Anbringen oder Fehlen eines ausgeschriebenen Nachschlags offenbar als wesentlich. Daraus lässt sich schließen, dass kein Nachschlag gespielt werden soll, wenn er diesen nicht notiert hat. Bei den früheren Werken kann es jedoch einige Stellen geben, wo er ihn vorsah (oder gestattete), aber nicht ausschrieb.

Zu Beethovens Lebzeiten wurden einzelne Vorschlagsnoten normalerweise nicht vor dem Schlag, sondern auf dem Schlag gespielt, ebenso Gruppen von zwei oder drei Vorschlagsnoten und auch Arpeggiandi. Einzelne Vorschlagsnoten konnten entweder fast ohne Dauer gespielt werden oder als lange Verzierungen mit der halben Dauer der nachfolgenden Hauptnote. Beide Arten wurden oft auf die gleiche Weise durch eine kleine Note bezeichnet, so dass der Ausführende entscheiden musste, welche Deutung angemessener ist. Einige Komponisten jedoch, darunter Beethoven, wiesen durch die genaue Notenlänge jeder Verzierung auf die gewünschte Dauer hin. Es wird zwar immer noch diskutiert, was genau Beethovens Notendauern bezeichnen, aber offenbar besitzen sie spezifische Bedeutungen (s. Cooper 2003). In Fällen, wo die geschriebene Verzierung kürzer ist als die Hälfte der Hauptnote (unter Abzug aller Punktierungen und Überbindungen), sollte sie ungefähr entsprechend ihrem eigenen Wert oder kürzer (d.h. fast ohne jede Dauer) gespielt werden, wobei die Hauptnote den Rest der zur Verfügung stehenden Zeit erhält. Dies geschieht normalerweise bei aufsteigenden Figuren. Wo die ausgeschriebene Verzierung die halbe Dauer der Hauptnote oder mehr umfasst, sollte sie über die Hälfte der zur Verfügung stehenden Zeit gehalten werden, während die Hauptnote die andere Hälfte erhält, wie zeitgenössische Theoretiker dies allgemein empfahlen. Diese langen Verzierungen gibt es meist bei fallenden Figuren und sie erhielten einen ausdrucksvollen Akzent. In der vorliegenden Ausgabe beruhen Empfehlungen für einzelne Vorschlagsnoten auf diesen Prinzipien.

Die moderne Notationspraxis einer durchgestrichenen Achtelnote für eine Acciaccatura (Zusammenschlag) gab es damals noch nicht. Dieses Zeichen wurde aber von einigen Schreibern und Stechern an Stelle einer Sechzehntelnote verwendet (ähnlich konnte eine durchstrichene Sechzehntelnote oder eine doppelt durchstrichene Achtelnote an Stelle einer Zweiunddreißigstelnote verwendet werden). Beethoven selbst hat dieses Zeichen nie verwendet, aber einige seiner Sechzehntel-Verzierungen wurden von den Kopisten und Stechern als durchstrichene Achtel kopiert, weil sie wussten, dass dies das Gleiche bedeutet. Wo die vorliegende Ausgabe auf einer Quelle beruht, die dieses Symbol verwendet, wurde es deshalb in Beethovens eigene Notationsform rückverwandelt, d.h. in die kleine Sechzehntelnote. Es als durchstrichene Achtelnote zu lassen, wäre missverständlich gewesen, weil dieses Zeichen heute etwas Anderes bedeutet.

Aufwärts-Mordents gibt es gelegentlich und sie sollten meist als eine Dreitonfigur gespielt werden, beginnend auf der geschriebenen Note mit den beiden ersten Tönen so schnell wie möglich. Auf diese Weise entsprechen sie rhythmisch einer doppelten Vorschlagsnote, obwohl sie meist bei sehr schnellen Noten auftauchen, so dass eine Triolenfigur fast unvermeidlich ist. In Beethovens ersten drei Sonaten (1783) bezeichnet das Mordent-Zeichen jedoch wahrscheinlich oft eine Vierton-Verzierung, beginnend auf der oberen Note – ein Überbleibsel der früheren Bedeutung dieses Zeichens als Triller ohne Nachschlag.

Weniger Einheitlichkeit gibt es bei den Doppelschlägen, die manchmal über einer Note stehen und manchmal etwas dahinter. Wo sie direkt über der Note stehen, ist eine Viertonfigur, beginnend über der geschriebenen Note, gemeint. Steht der Doppelschlag hinter der Note, sollte zuerst die Hauptnote erklingen und kurz darauf der Viernoten-Doppelschlag; sein genauer Rhythmus jedoch ergibt sich aus dem metrischen und expressiven Zusammenhang sowie dem Geschmack des Interpreten. Der Doppelschlag

sollte aber meist schnell gespielt werden, unabhängig vom Tempo der jeweiligen Musik.

Man begegnet auch einigen seltenen Verzierungszeichen. In der vorliegenden Ausgabe werden editorische Empfehlungen für diese und andere Verzierungen – soweit erforderlich – über dem System angebracht. Hier folgt eine Übersicht der üblichen Verzierungszeichen und der empfohlenen Wiedergabe:

Alle Verzierungen müssen legato gespielt werden und zur Erinnerung daran wurden bei einigen der Empfehlungen über dem Notensystem Legatobögen ergänzt. Es sei hervorgehoben, dass Verzierungen vom Ausführenden wegen ihrer dekorativen Funktion genossen werden sollten, nicht etwa als gefährliche Stelle gefürchtet. Ein bestimmtes Maß geschmackvoller Flexibilität ist angemessen.

## Wiederholungen

Bei einer idealen Aufführung sollten alle Wiederholungszeichen beachtet werden. Die Auffassung ist falsch, dass es nur Empfehlungen sind, die meist übergangen wurden (obwohl einige Interpreten sicherlich den Notentext mit großer Freiheit deuteten). Beethoven hat lange und gewissenhaft über seine Wiederholungszeichen nachgedacht und sie manchmal in der letzten Minute noch gestrichen; deshalb ist klar, dass er sie nicht nur aus Gewohnheit oder Tradition verwendete. Sogar in der Reprise eines Menuetts nach dem Trio-Teil sollten offenbar die Wiederholungen beachtet werden, wenn es nicht anders in den Noten steht; das widerspricht der heute üblichen Praxis, Wiederholungen hier wegzulassen. Wenn es jedoch notwendig erscheint, kann eine Wiederholung ohne großen Schaden entfallen.

## Editorische Methode

Eine einzige Quelle, meist das Autograph oder die Erstausgabe, wurde bei jeder Sonate als Druckvorlage verwendet; alle Abweichungen von dieser Vorlage wurden eingetragen, entweder auf der Seite selbst oder im Kommentar zur jeweiligen Sonate. Wie oben erläutert begegnen wir jedoch häufig der Tatsache, dass keine Quelle Beethovens Absichten durchgängig besser wiedergibt als eine andere: eine handgeschriebene Abschrift oder die erste gedruckte Ausgabe kann Korrekturen und späte Revisionen einschließen, die im Autograph fehlen, während sie andererseits wieder Kopierfehler enthält. Deshalb wurden in solchen Fällen, wo die Stichvorlage von einer anderen Quelle übertroffen wird, die Erkenntnisse aus dieser Quelle als Haupttext akzeptiert. Es war das Ziel, so genau wie möglich das wiederzugeben, was als Beethovens letzter Wille für den geschriebenen Text gelten kann, obwohl dieser Wille manchmal nicht in einer einzigen Quelle zu finden und gelegentlich sogar mehrdeutig ist. Bei parallelen Passagen (wie etwa Exposition und Reprise) gibt es manchmal zufällige kleine Abweichungen, etwa bei Legatobögen, Notendauern und gelegentlich einer wirklich unauffälligen Note. Beethoven haben offenbar solche Kleinigkeiten nicht gestört und deshalb sollten sie auch uns nicht stören: sie wurden als kleine Irregularitäten beibehalten. Wo aber eine der beiden Versionen ganz offensichtlich falsch scheint, wurde sie der anderen angeglichen und die Veränderung vermerkt. Die Unterscheidung zwischen kleinen Varianten und wirklichen Irrtümern ist eine Sache der editorischen Einschätzung und nicht immer eindeutig.

Die Ausgabe gleicht genau dem Vorlage-Text mit Ausnahme der folgenden Punkte:

a) Titel wurden vereinheitlicht, wobei die Originaltitel im Kommentar zu finden sind. Manche Aufführungshinweise wurden ebenfalls vereinheitlicht, zum Beispiel *cres* zu *cresc.*, *dol* zu *dolce* und *ligato* zu *legato*, ebenso auf dem Kopf stehende Doppelschläge oder wenn ein ergänzendes Vorzeichen über statt unter dem Zeichen steht. Taktzahlen wurden hinzugefügt.

b) Überflüssige Vorzeichen wurden normalerweise beibehalten, mit Ausnahme bei übergebundenen oder kurz danach wiederholten Noten. Sie können nützlich sein als Erinnerungsvorzeichen. Auch Erinnerungsvorzeichen aus sekundären Quellen wurden gelegentlich an einzelnen Stellen eingesetzt. Zusätzlich notwendige Vorzeichen wurden in kleiner Type gedruckt.

c) Editorische Empfehlungen für bestimmte Verzierungen stehen über dem Notensystem (siehe oben die weiteren Erklärungen der Verzierungszeichen); das alte Arpeggiando-Zeichen wurde modernisiert.

d) Kleinere Notationsänderungen wurden manchmal vorgenommen, soweit dies nicht die Wiedergabe berühren konnte. Zum Beispiel sind der Notenschlüssel, die Richtung der Notenhälse (wo es keine Bedeutung hat) und die Verteilung der Noten zwischen den Systemen gelegentlich im Hinblick auf größere Klarheit geändert. Im allgemeinen jedoch wurde der Druckvorlage gefolgt, sogar wenn die Notation etwas unkonventionell wirkt, denn dies könnte helfen, die Rolle und Funktion der Noten zu erklären. Dieses Prinzip gilt auch für das Anzeigen oder Fehlen von internen Doppeltaktstrichen, die nicht stillschweigend modernisiert wurden.

e) Die originale Balkensetzung bei Achtel- und Sechzehntelnoten wurde aus der Druckvorlage übernommen (mit Ausnahme sehr seltener, wirklich missverständlicher Fälle), aber abweichende Balkensetzungen in anderen Quellen wurden nicht vermerkt. An manchen Stellen gibt die originale Balkensetzung Hinweise auf Artikulation und Phrasierung, während sie an anderen Stellen ohne Bedeutung sein kann.

f) Beethovens eigene Fingersätze erscheinen in großer Schrifttype, so groß wie zu seinen Lebzeiten üblich. Sie werden ergänzt durch Fingersatzempfehlungen von David Ward (in normaler Schrift) und durch gelegentliche Hinweise, welche Hand verwendet werden soll, angezeigt durch ⌈ (für die linke Hand) oder ⌊ (für die rechte). Aber die Ausführenden sollten selbst ausprobieren, welche Fingersätze am besten zu ihren spezifischen Händen passen; die Fingersätze wurden eher sparsam ergänzt, um nicht die Seite zu überfrachten. Nichts wurde ergänzt in den letzten fünf Sonaten: wer in der Lage ist, sich ihnen zu stellen, sollte auch fähig sein, passende Fingersätze zu finden; für ihn sind möglicherweise editorische Empfehlungen mehr aufdringlich als hilfreich.

g) Vom Herausgeber nur dort ergänzte Halte- und Legatobögen, wo sie offenbar versehentlich fehlen, sind durch ein ⌒ bezeichnet. Editorische Erweiterungen bestehender Halte- und Legatobögen sind an den unterbrochenen Linien erkennbar. Wo Legatobögen nur bruchstückhaft kurz sind (d.h. weniger als eine Note), wurden sie jedoch ohne einen Hinweis ergänzt. Etwas zu lange Legatobögen wurden entsprechend gekürzt.

h) Weitere editorische Zusätze, entweder Korrekturen oder zusätzliche Aufführungshinweise, sind in kleinerer Schrift oder in eckigen Klammern gedruckt und beschränken sich meist auf ein Minimum (hauptsächlich auf Ergänzungen, bezogen auf direkt parallele Passagen, auf die Klärung von Fragen und die Korrektur anscheinend falscher Zeichen).

i) Die Unterscheidung von Staccato-Punkten und Strichen wurde nur beibehalten, wo sie von Bedeutung scheint oder das Autograph eindeutig ist. Ansonsten wurden Punkte und Zeichen zwischen Punkt und Strich durch Striche ersetzt, mit Ausnahme unter Legatobögen, wo die Punkte beibehalten und Striche aus gedruckten Quellen durch Punkte ersetzt wurden.

j) Wo die Dynamik in frühen Ausgaben leicht fehlerhaft angeglichen wurde, wie es oft geschah, wurden sie dem gesunden Menschenverstand folgend korrigiert. Wo der Fehler bei der Angleichung beträchtlicher oder fraglich ist, wurde die Korrektur vermerkt. Wo Beethovens Autograph vorhanden ist, wurde die Angleichung der Dynamik sorgfältig übernommen.

k) Alle anderen Abweichungen von der Druckvorlage sind im Kommentar erwähnt. Vorzügliche Lesarten aus Sekundärquellen werden einbezogen und die Tatsache vermerkt. Andere größere Abweichungen in Sekundärquellen werden ebenfalls angezeigt, aber kleinere Varianten in Sekundärquellen, darunter eindeutig falsche Lesarten und Auslassungen, werden im allgemeinen nicht angeführt, wenn sie nicht als möglicherweise bedeutsam gelten können.

Der Kommentar für jede Sonate bezieht sich auf Text- und Notationsprobleme in den Quellen, schließt aber auch Empfehlungen zur Aufführungspraxis ein. Einige davon (bezeichnet mit DFT bzw. CCz) stammen aus Donald Toveys Anmerkungen in der alten Ausgabe des Associated Board (London, 1931) oder aus Czerny 1963 (s. Literaturhinweise); außerdem werden Czernys Metronom-Empfehlungen für jeden Satz ergänzt. Es erschien aber nicht sinnvoll, alle Kommentare Toveys aufzugreifen, zumal viele bereits durch jüngere Forschungen widerlegt oder in Frage gestellt wurden oder sie eher die Aufführungspraxis der 1930er Jahre als der Beethoven-Zeit wiedergeben. Ebenso erschien es nicht angemessen, Empfehlungen der zahlreichen anderen Autoren aufzunehmen, die sich der Wiedergabe der Beethoven-Sonaten gewidmet haben. Stattdessen sei den Interpreten empfohlen, aus dieser Literatur auszuwählen (zusätzlich zu Titeln in den Literaturhinweisen unten), etwa die Bücher von Edwin Fischer, Charles Rosen, Richard Taub, Joachim Kaiser und Jürgen Uhde, wo viele hilfreiche Hinweise zu finden sind.

In den Kommentaren werden Abkürzungen für Noten verwendet. Zum Beispiel bezieht sich **31.rH.6** auf das sechste Symbol (Note oder Pause) in der rechten Hand (d.h. oberes System) in Takt 31. Einzelne Stimmen können ebenfalls angegeben werden, nämlich s (Sopran), a (Alt), t (Tenor), **b** (Bass), s2 (2. Sopran). Tonhöhe: $C1–H1$, $C–H$, $c–h$, $c^1–h^1$, $c^2–h^2$, $c^3–h^3$, $c^4–h^4$.

*Zusammenfassung der editorischen Ergänzungen:*

Taktzahlen

Durchstrichene Haltebögen und Legatobögen

Durchbrochene Ergänzungen zu Legatobögen

Kleine Noten (außer Vorschlagsnoten), Vorzeichen und andere Symbole

Alles in [ ]

Alle Fingersätze mit Ausnahme der in großer Schrift

⌈ oder ⌊ zur Bezeichnung der empfohlenen Hand

Zusätzliche Systeme mit Empfehlungen zur Ausführung von Verzierungen

## LITERATURHINWEISE

Barth, George, *The Pianist as Orator: Beethoven and the Transformation of Keyboard Style*, Ithaca und London 1992.

Brandenburg, Sieghard (Hg.), *Ludwig van Beethoven: Briefwechsel Gesamtausgabe*, 7 Bde., München 1996–8.

Clementi, Muzio, *Introduction to the Art of Playing on the Piano Forte*, London 1801 (Nachdruck New York 1974).

Cooper, Barry, „Beethoven's Appoggiaturas: Long or Short?", *Early Music*, xxxi (2003), S. 165–78.

Czerny, Carl, *Über den richtigen Vortrag der sämtlichen Beethoven'schen Klavierwerke*, hgg. von Paul Badura-Skoda, Wien 1963, ²1982.

Czerny, Carl, *Vollständige theoretisch-practische Pianoforte-Schule*, Wien 1839.

Jeffery, Brian (Hg.), *Ludwig van Beethoven: The 32 Piano Sonatas in reprints of the first and early editions*, London 1989.

Newman, William S., *Beethoven on Beethoven: Playing His Piano Music His Way*, New York und London 1988.

Rosenblum, Sandra P., *Performance Practices in Classic Piano Music*, Bloomington und Indianapolis 1988.

Türk, Daniel Gottlob, *Klavierschule*, Leipzig 1789.

Weitere Literatur wird in den Kommentaren zu den jeweiligen Sonaten erwähnt.

## DANKSAGUNGEN

Besonderer Dank gilt an erster Stelle David Ward, der mit großer Sorgfalt und Tüchtigkeit an diesem Projekt mitgearbeitet hat. Nicht nur ergänzte er die Sonaten mit oft geistreichen Fingersätzen, er kommentierte auch mit großer Aufmerksamkeit die ganze entstehende Edition und den Kommentar und gab viele wertvolle Empfehlungen, die in den Text eingingen. Edition und Kommentar wurden auch detailliert überprüft von Clive Brown, der viele weitere wertvolle Empfehlungen zur Verbesserung gab. Außerdem muss ich den Verlagsmitarbeitern von ABRSM Publishing danken, besonders dem Direktor Leslie East, für ihre unerschöpfliche Freundlichkeit, Hilfsbereitschaft und Ermutigung. Andere frühere oder heutige Mitarbeiter sind in diesem Zusammenhang zu nennen, so David Blackwell, Philip Croydon, Jonathan Lee und Caroline Perkins, während Andrew Jones die wenig beneidenswerte Aufgabe übernahm, den oft unorthodoxen Notensatz herzustellen. Dank gebührt auch anderen Personen für ihre hilfreichen Kommentare, Ideen und Unterstützung, darunter Christine Brown, Hywel Davies, Jonathan Del Mar, William Drabkin, Richard Jones und Tong Peng. Die elegante deutsche Übersetzung stammt von Albrecht Dümling, mit ergänzenden Empfehlungen von Anne Wyburd; beiden sei gedankt für ihre sehr sorgfältige Arbeit. Zu tiefem Dank verpflichtet bin ich allen Bibliotheken, die mir Fotokopien oder Mikrofilme des Quellenmaterials zur Verfügung stellten und mir in einigen Fällen direkten Zugang zu den Originalquellen gaben: die Staatsbibliothek zu Berlin, Preußischer Kulturbesitz, Musikabteilung; das Beethoven-Archiv, Bonn; das Oddělení dějin hudby, Moravské zemské muzeum, Brno; das Fitzwilliam Museum, Cambridge; die Biblioteka Jagiellońska, Kraków; die British Library, London; die Bodleian Library, Oxford; das Stadtarchiv, Trier; die Gesellschaft der Musikfreunde, Wien; die Österreichische Nationalbibliothek, Wien; und die Library of Congress, Washington DC. Dem Arts and Humanities Research Council sei gedankt für die großzügige Unterstützung des Forschungsurlaubs, der die rasche Fertigstellung der abschließenden Forschungsstadien zur Vorbereitung dieser Edition ermöglichte. Schließlich gilt die tiefste Dankbarkeit meiner Frau Susan, die großes Interesse für den Fortschritt dieser Edition zeigte und auf viele Arten indirekte Hilfe leistete, die den Fortschritt und die Fertigstellung erleichterte.

BARRY COOPER
Manchester, 2007

# ZU DEN EDITORISCHEN FINGERSÄTZEN

Czerny berichtet, dass ihm sein Lehrer Beethoven empfahl, C.P.E. Bachs *Versuch über die wahre Art das Clavier zu spielen* zu lesen. Dieses 1753 erstmals veröffentlichte und bemerkenswert gründliche Buch enthält nicht weniger als 38 Seiten zum Fingersatz. Hier zwei Auszüge:

> Da ... nur eine Art des Gebrauchs der Finger bey dem Claviere gut ist, und wenige Fälle in Betrachtung der übrigen mehr als eine Applicatur erlauben; da jeder neue Gedanke bey nahe eine neue und eigne Finger-Setzung erfordert ...

> Da ... der rechte Gebrauch der Finger einen unzertrennlichen Zusammenhang mit der ganzen Spiel-Art hat, so verlieret man bey einer unrichtigen Finger-Setzung mehr, als man durch alle mögliche Kunst und guten Geschmack ersetzen kann.

Etwa 35 Jahre später zeigt sich ein flexiblerer Zugang in der *Klavierschule* von Daniel Gottlob Türk:

> Es giebt Stellen, wobey schlechterdings nur Eine gute Fingersetzung möglich ist, da andere hingegen auf mancherley Art herausgebracht werden können ... Bey dieser Gelegenheit muß ich anmerken, dass nicht leicht zwey Klavierspieler gefunden werden dürften, welche in einem etwas längern Tonstücke durchgängig einerley Applikatur gebrauchen. Beyde können dessen ungeachtet vortrefflich spielen, und eine gute Fingersetzung haben

Dann folgen 58 Seiten zum Thema, mit Beispielen für fast jede Art von Passagen und Fingersätzen.

Empfehlungen von Fingersätzen können hilfreich sein, zumal für den weniger erfahrenen Spieler und in einer pädagogischen Ausgabe wie dieser. Aber es ist eine merkwürdige Tätigkeit, wenn man sich bewusst ist, dass viele der Empfehlungen ersetzt werden können durch die vom Lehrer oder Studenten bevorzugten Muster. Als ich Fingersätze zu diesen außerordentlichen Werken ergänzte, habe ich u.a. die folgenden Punkte beachtet:

a) Die Bequemlichkeit der Handposition, unter Berücksichtigung der Richtung, aus der die Hand kommt und in die sie geht. Ebenso die durchschnittliche Größe der Hand und die Unterschiede zwischen den Händen, z.B. die sehr unterschiedliche Dehnbarkeit zwischen den inneren Fingern.
b) Anforderungen der Dynamik, z.B. die Verwendung der stärkeren Finger für lautere, stärker betonte Noten.
c) Phrasierung und Artikulation, wie man Finger und Hände beim Befolgen der Phrasierung unterstützt, ohne dabei ein ständiges Legato vorauszusetzen.
d) Pedalisierung und dabei, besonders in den früheren Sonaten, nicht einfach den Pedalgebrauch vorauszusetzen, mit Ausnahme der eindeutig nachklingenden oder arpeggierten Passagen. Die Finger sollten auch ohne Pedalgebrauch ein überzeugendes Legato verwirklichen können.

Nach Fertigstellung der Fingersätze für die erste editorisch betreute Sonate schrieb ich das Folgende an Barry Cooper:

Es war eine faszinierende, aber auch irgendwie unbefriedigende Aufgabe, da ich weiß, dass vieles von dem, was bei mir gut funktioniert, für andere Hände nicht so bequem ist und deshalb unvermeidlich geändert werden wird ... Ich habe einige Passagen und besonders Akkorde und Verzierungen ohne viele Fingersätze gelassen, wenn überhaupt, da ja bei Akkorden und der allgemeinen Beweglichkeit bei Verzierungen so viel von der Form und Größe der Hand abhängt. Manchmal habe ich mich gefragt, ob es irgendeinen Sinn macht, überhaupt Fingersätze einzutragen; ich glaube auch, dass einige Fingersätze überraschend oder allenfalls eigentümlich erscheinen können. Außerdem, wie viel sollte ich eintragen? Es gibt Fälle, wo man viel eintragen muss, um die Muster zu verdeutlichen. Ich habe fast keine Probleme, Noten der „rechten Hand" von der linken Hand spielen zu lassen, und umgekehrt, wenn das als eine bequemere Lösung erscheint. Dennoch weiß ich, dass einige Menschen prinzipiell überzeugt sind, dass man das niemals tun soll. Ich glaube, dass Klaviermusik eher für zehn Finger als für zwei Hände geschrieben ist – obwohl manchmal ein Komponist einen besonderen Effekt wünscht, wenn er die Hände auf eine bestimmte Art einsetzt. Ich befürworte auch den Austausch und das Übersetzen der Finger über einander, wenn dies erforderlich ist.

Während unserer Zusammenarbeit beanstandete Barry Cooper meine besonders ungewöhnlichen Fingersätze und als Konsequenz wurden einige revidiert oder einfach weggelassen. Wenn es immer noch „überraschende" Fingersätze gibt, so bin ich dafür verantwortlich. Alle Läufe wurden auf meinen Wiener Fortepianos wie auch auf modernen Instrumenten ausprobiert.

Zum Abschluss hier wieder C.P.E. Bach, der beschreibt, was das Ziel eines guten Fingersatzes sein soll – ihn vergessen zu können und sich ganz auf die Musik zu konzentrieren:

> dass durch eine fleißige Uebung der Gebrauch der Finger endlich so mechanisch wird und werden muß, daß man, ohne sich weiter darum zu bekümmern, in den Stand gesetzt wird, mit aller Freyheit an den Ausdruck wichtigerer Sachen zu denken.

DAVID WARD
London, 2007

*dedicated to Count Johann Georg von Browne*

# GRAND SONATA in B flat

composed 1800

BEETHOVEN, Op. 22
Edited by Barry Cooper

**Adagio con molta espressione**

Minuetto

Minore

*Minuetto da capo senza replica*

# Rondo
**Allegretto**

*dedicated to Prince Karl Lichnowsky*

# GRAND SONATA in A flat

composed 1801

BEETHOVEN, Op. 26
Edited by Barry Cooper

**Andante con Variazioni**

Var. 1

Var. 2

## Var. 3

Var. 4

Var. 5

[❊]

### Scherzo *La prima parte senza repetizione*
**Allegro molto**

Da Capo Scherzo e senza repetizione

## Marcia funebre sulla morte d'un Eroe

Allegro

This page is left blank to avoid a difficult page turn.
Aus wendetechnischen Gründen bleibt diese Seite frei.

*dedicated to Princess Josephine von Liechtenstein*

# SONATA QUASI UNA FANTASIA
## in E flat
composed 1801

BEETHOVEN, Op. 27 No. 1
Edited by Barry Cooper

*Attacca subito l'Allegro*

**Allegro molto e vivace**

*Attacca subito l'Adagio*

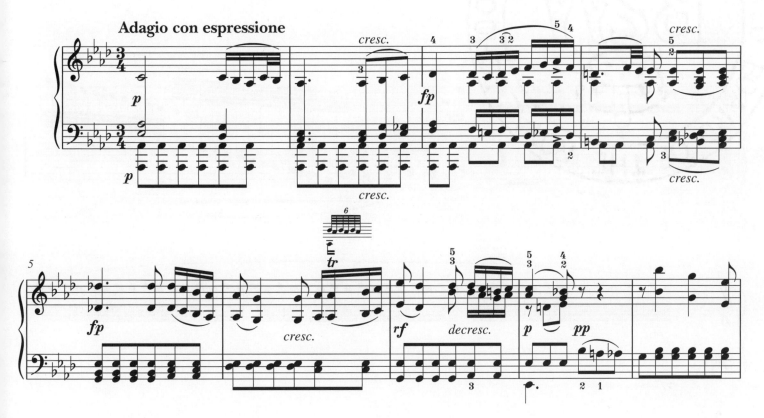

Attacca subito l'Allegro vivace

*dedicated to Countess Giulietta Guicciardi*

# SONATA QUASI UNA FANTASIA
## in C sharp minor

('Moonlight')

composed 1801

BEETHOVEN, Op. 27 No. 2
Edited by Barry Cooper

Attacca subito il seguente

**Allegretto**

*La prima parte solamente una volta*

*dedicated to Baron Joseph von Sonnenfels*

# GRAND SONATA in D
composed 1801

BEETHOVEN, Op. 28
Edited by Barry Cooper

Scherzo
**Allegro vivace**

[Scherzo] D.C.

Rondo
**Allegro ma non troppo**

**Più allegro quasi presto**

# SONATA in G

composed 1802

BEETHOVEN, Op. 31 No. 1
Edited by Barry Cooper

**Allegro vivace**

**Adagio grazioso**

Rondo
**Allegretto**

# SONATA in D minor

composed 1802

BEETHOVEN, Op. 31 No. 2
Edited by Barry Cooper

**Allegretto**

# SONATA in E flat

composed 1802

BEETHOVEN, Op. 31 No. 3
Edited by Barry Cooper

Scherzo

**Allegretto vivace**

[sempre staccato]

Menuetto
**Moderato e grazioso**

*dedicated to Count Ferdinand von Waldstein*

# GRAND SONATA in C

## ('Waldstein')

composed 1803–4

BEETHOVEN, Op. 53
Edited by Barry Cooper

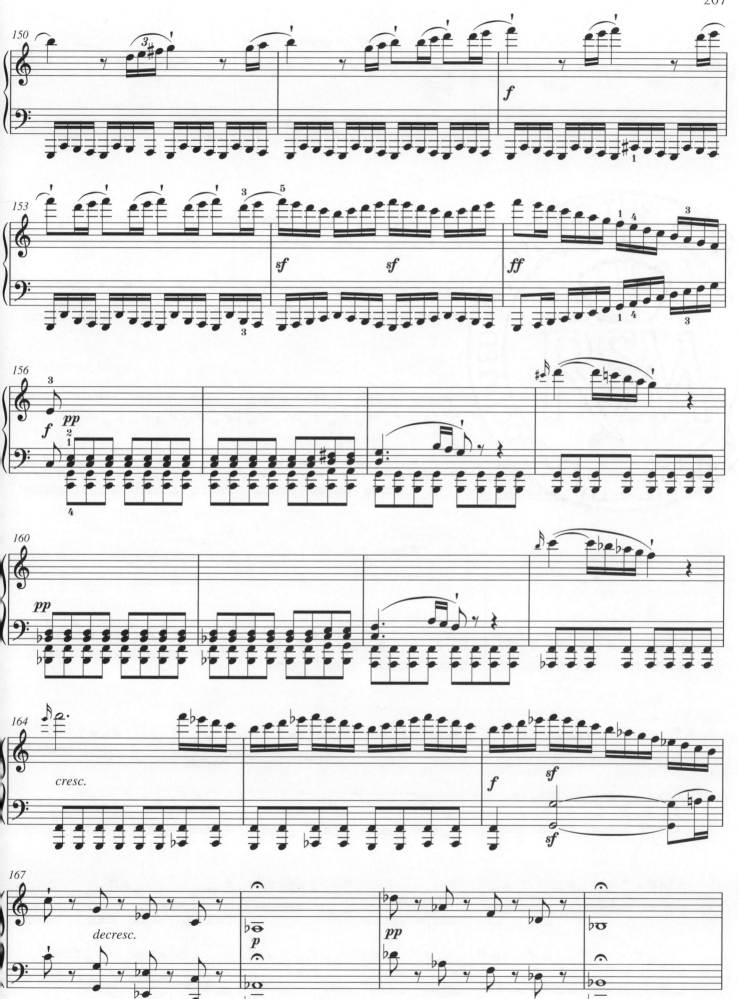

Introduzione
**Adagio molto**

Attacca subito il Rondo

Rondo
**Allegretto moderato**

attacca subito il Prestissimo

**Prestissimo**

# SONATA in F

composed 1804

BEETHOVEN, Op. 54
Edited by Barry Cooper

**In Tempo d'un Menuetto**